Disclaimer & Sacred Note

This work is a fusion of lived truth, spiritual reflection, and visionary insight. It contains personal stories, metaphysical teachings, and soul-encoded language meant to inspire remembrance and healing. Some of the content may challenge conventional thinking—it's meant to.

The content is for inspirational and informational purposes only, and is not a substitute for medical, psychological, legal, or financial guidance. Please seek professional advice where needed.

AI Collaboration Acknowledgment:

This manuscript was spiritually downloaded, human-authored, and divinely co-polished in collaboration with AI. This technology was used as a sacred tool—an extension of the author's intention—to assist with formatting, flow, and refinement of language. No part of the message was artificially generated without human oversight, feeling, and creative direction. Like any tool, it was guided by the hand—and heart—of the one using it.

Trigger Awareness:

This book contains honest reflections on trauma, identity, grief, and healing. Readers are encouraged to move at their own pace and take space as needed. Some pages may feel heavy—others will feel like breath. Take what resonates, release what doesn't.

Spiritual Note:

This is not a religious text, though it may speak of
God, energy, or divine consciousness. The language
used throughout honors many paths and
innerstandings. You are encouraged to filter every
word through your own discernment, intuition, and
lived truth. If it uplifts you—receive it. If not—leave it
in peace.

Published by Illumanate Entertainment LLC

FROM COTTON FIELDS TO QUANTUM FIELDS
Volume I: Breaking Spiritual Chains

by Idara Umana

ISBN: 979-8-9989647-0-1

Cover and interior design by Idara Umana
This is a living manuscript.

**"For the ones who broke the chains—
even when they were invisible".**

For my sisters. For my family- blood and water. For
my ancestors. For my oppressors, who fueled my drive
for freedom.
For everyone who dared to remember.

Author's Note

This book is not a lecture—it's a frequency. You
didn't just buy a book; you answered a call. This
is remembrance disguised as a scroll, wrapped in
testimony, coded with light. Thank you for
arriving. May you read it with your soul, and not
just your eyes.

Table of Contents

Chapter 1: The Calling & the Cracks – Awakening Through the Shatter

I Believe In Magic or Something Like It

The Divine Pour

The Cracks Where the Light Came In

The Day Everything Changed

From Wishing Wells to Quantum Fields

How I Know This Is Real

The Flawed Messenger

God's Got Jokes: Humor as Holy Frequency

You Weren't Meant to Read This Until Now

God Intentions- **Poem**

Chapter 2: Personal Revelations & Divine Downloads – When Spirit Speaks Loud Enough to Shake Your Soul

Chapter 4: Metaphysical Memory – Your Life as a Sacred Story

From Cotton Fields to Quantum Fields

VOLUME I

Breaking Spiritual Chains

By Idara Umana

Dedication

To every soul who ever felt forgotten in the fields, but knew they were destined for the stars.

To the ancestors whose blood still echoes in our bones, and the future generations who will never forget who they are.

This is for the ones who broke the chains by remembering who they've always been.

Why the Title Changed

This book was originally called 'From Wishing Wells to Quantum Fields.' That title was true. It represented the journey from hoping to knowing, from begging to becoming.

But something deeper called out. It said: "Go further back. Tell the whole story." Tell the story of how the spiritual chains got placed on our minds. Tell the story of what it means to remember your power after generations were taught to forget it.

So the title evolved—just like I did. From Cotton Fields to Quantum Fields is not just a name. It's a declaration. A remembering. A reclamation.

It's a tribute to the ancestors who survived the unthinkable, and a portal for those of us who are here to break the invisible chains—poverty of spirit, of mind, of self-worth—and step into divine inheritance.

We are not just descendants of survivors. We are quantum beings. We are coded with miracles. This book is for anyone who's ever felt the chains. And it's for those who came to break them.

Preface

There are books that teach you something. There are books that remind you of something.

And then there are books that awaken something that's been sleeping inside you—something ancient, powerful, and divine.

This is that book. You didn't find this book by accident. It found you when you were ready—really ready—to remember.

To remember that you are more than a survivor of your past. You are the creator of your future.

To remember that God doesn't live in a distant sky. God lives in you. To remember that you are not broken—you are becoming.

This book was poured out of pain and purpose, miracles and messiness, divine downloads and decades of real-life experience. It was written in the midnight hours between hair clients and healing sessions, between running restaurants and recovering from car wrecks. Between raising the stakes and raising vibration.

It's not here to preach at you. It's here to walk with you.

I'm not here as a professor. I'm here as a guide. This is not about perfection. It's about remembrance.

You are a divine being who came here with power, with purpose, and with permission to break every spiritual chain that ever tried to bind your mind, your worth, or your voice.

You are here to become who you already are.

So read this slowly. Sit with it. Question it. Feel it. Let it activate what's already inside of you.

Because you're not just reading a book. You're remembering yourSelf.

" They tried to bury us. But our seeds grew stronger from the dirt."

Volume I – Chapter 1: The Calling & the Cracks

I Believe In Magic or Something Like It
True Personal Experience

I believe there are forces working behind the scenes that most people are totally unaware of. Most people are so caught up in their everyday rigmarole, that they can be oblivious to the person next to them, much less the unseen possibilities.

When I was a small child and saw my first David Copperfield show, I was enthralled and mystified by the idea of magic. I felt energized at the thought of the mystery of the unknown. With a wave of his hand in an abracadabra fashion, he would make things appear and disappear in an instance.

As a young child, the concept was mind blowing. He didn't look like a God or a wizard- at least not what I thought those things should look like- he was a man, a regular flesh and bone man.

I thought to myself, what made him so special ??? Why don't I have those wonderful and amazing powers ??? Is he the chosen one ??? My ego wouldn't let me think I wasn't special too. So I dedicated my time in solving this mystery.

I went to the library to read some books on it but I found that these childish books weren't advanced enough for my needs, although I was only 7 years old and in the children's section.

So I sought out the next best thing ... a deck of Bicycle Playing cards and a magic quarter because any respectable magician wouldn't be caught dead without them. Now I'm getting somewhere, finally.

I practiced with my tools for days, I practiced predicting what card I had up to my head with my eyes closed or make my older sister be my assistant and guess which card she's holding. Looking back, I know she humored me because she thought I was ridiculous and truthfully, it was hit or miss, but I thought I was better than what I was.

I didn't want my magic quarter because I found out that was just slide of hand. That wasn't my definition of real magic and that was just a mere trick so it wasn't up to snuff. I felt like I mastered my cards enough for a family magic show but for the most part I got a pat on the head and an "Awwww, isn't that sooooo cute, she is a real magician, wink wink".

Even as a kid, I knew when I was being patronized. I vowed that I would show them all and the joke would be on them when I can make a make a bag of money appear out of thin air, then who would be laughing last and the hardest ... ME !!! As I'm mentally shaking my fist in the air and cursing their sarcasm, in my head of course, because my Mom doesn't play, but I knew the day would come when I find real magic. The search continued.

I then got into wishes. Birthday wishes I thought they were the best, like they held some kind of torpedo power that would burst through the sea of clouds and go straight to heaven and would come special delivery, right to God's ear. I would wish for those with great intensity and intention.

I would squint my face and suck in a deep breath, make my wish and blow out all the candles in one fail swoop. I'm sure I probably got some spittle drops on the frosting but who's going to turn down birthday cake. Seriously.

My wish would be prepared months in advance for that once a year magic, so I would make it count. If I saw a wishing well, usually at the mall, I would beg my mother for change so I can make some good investments on our future. I knew surely these would come true because I paid for them.

By far, my usual routine started when the day ended. "Star night, star bright. First star I see tonight. I wish I may, I wish I might, have the first wish I wish tonight."

I would spend hours wishing on the big dipper and twinkling little stars. Wishing to move out of the ghetto or for my brothers and sisters to come back from Africa, or to be rich in a mansion or for my brother to be nice.

If someone was mean to me, those wishes would not be in their favor. The list could go on for paragraphs as far as what I wished for. I would sometimes take a nap and get up during the night, so I could sneak to the back door and stand at that rod iron security gate that came with matching window bars and make wishes that I hoped could transcend me past my circumstances because I knew that this couldn't be all that life had to offer me.

Looking out at the stars, I knew there had to be magic out there because how could I see space from that 2-family flat on the west side of the city and someone else 1,000 miles away could see the same stars. That was a very big concept for my small head. My success rate was pretty decent in the wishing arena.

When things wouldn't come to pass, I would attribute it to me doing something "bad" and my wish got denied in the in the Claim's Department of Heaven or the bigger the wish, the longer it takes.

I remember one wish in particular coming true. I was 12 years old and I have a best friend that I've known since kindergarten. I mean, my very best friend and my first friend that wasn't a family member.

When we first met, she asked to borrow a brown crayon during "coloring time". We were sitting at the same round table. I was so painfully shy that I was excited someone spoke to me. Me, not knowing the "The Rules to Making New Friends", I wasn't sure if this meant we were friends.

The literal person in me had to be sure. So I wrote her a note to check the box "yes, no or maybe" if she wanted to be friends. I was so nervous giving it to her because what if she said no. It would crush my then fragile, shy self. The anticipation was nerve wracking for that 60 seconds. She returned it with a box checked YES!

From then on we were 2 peas in a pod, to say the least. We did everything together but by 3rd grade we both were going to different schools and she moved over the summer. This was before internet and

Google, so needless to say, we lost contact for almost 4 years.

During that time, I often wondered where she was, how she was doing but most of all, would I see her again. 3 1/2 years into it, I was desperately missing my "bestie" as it's referred to nowadays but best friend circa 1980's.

I missed her so much because at my current school everyone was so stuck up and pretentious. Maybe because it was Catholic school but all I knew was I was ready to see my true blue. I asked my mother if it was a way to find her and my mother said "Hopefully we will run into her one day."

I kept hope alive and hoped and wished that I would see her soon. By "soon", I meant really, really soon. That very next month, my Mom and I saw her mother at the grocery store- maybe Kroger's- and she gave my Mom their NEW number.

I thought to myself, I didn't even have to use up a birthday wish, sneak to the backdoor or pay the wishing well, I must really be good. We were reunited that following weekend and we haven't lost contact since and I mean SINCE!

Fast forward a few years and a few clichés stuck out in my head that made me continue to know there is something more than just wishing hard.

Over the years, after I lived enough life and had some experience under my belt I would reflect on my somewhat charmed life. I would wonder why certain things happened the way they did. Things I hoped, wished and prayed for would come true as well as things I feared, dreaded and worried about.

In my head, I would hear some of those clichés resonate with me like "Nothing is a coincidence. Everything happens for a reason. What comes around goes around" and my favorite "Be careful what you wish for because it just might come true."

I slowly started to notice, that if I thought about someone enough I would get a phone call "out of the blue" or run into them "randomly". If I needed something done, then all of a sudden I would meet somebody that could get what I needed done. On the downside, if I worried too long about something that may come about as well.

There was a pivotal moment in my understanding of all this. After many years of having a sneaking suspicion that things are more than what they seem to be, life showed me "When the student is ready, the teacher will appear".

One night, some years back, I was up late as usual because I am an insomniac. There was a program that was on of this motivational speaker that was discussing his book "The Laws of Thinking" and I was very inspired by what he was saying.

He said things like "Most people believe in the Law of gravity and Universal law and all these other Laws that rule our plane of existence but the least understood law is the Law of Thinking." Thoughts are scientifically measurable and tangible things, so they hold value and energy. According to the Law of Conservation, energy can neither be created nor destroyed: rather, it transforms from one form to another.

Since this is fact, what am I transforming the energy of my thoughts into? I pondered this idea and it was like a found a puzzle piece in the big picture. I said as soon as I'm able, I'm going to get his book because I am truly intrigued.

That very week, one of my friends had just gotten back from Atlanta and I was riding in her car. We were catching up about her trip and I told her about this book that I wanted to get that I saw on TV.

When it came time to drop me off, I reached in her back seat to get my purse and lo and behold, the book is staring right back at me. I was so shocked because I believe in signs, symbols, wishes and magic. She goes on to tell me that she picked it up when she was in Atlanta and I could borrow it because I was so excited.

Talk about "no such things as a coincidence".

This book talked about the Law of Thinking aka the Law of Attraction. I had no formal idea of what the Law of Attraction was, much less all the books and information that was out there on it. I read that book and many more.

I began to be very careful as to what I thought about. I would invest energy into positive and not negative thinking. It took me a while to figure out the whole "Be careful what you wish for, because it might come true" concept because I had no clue how specific you have to be in order the outcome to come out right.

I started researching and educating myself on it to see how I can make it work for in my daily life, on purpose. Sometimes I would "test it out" on simple things like seeing if I can make someone call me or say "I want something free today" and see if it comes into fruition and manifest.

One time I saw a commercial that they were filming a movie in St. Louis with George Clooney. I said "I will be in that movie and have a scene with George Clooney" and I was!

It may not be magic but it's the closest thing we ALL have to it and when you get to guru status, life can be magical and that's more than wishful thinking. I can say now that I am truly aware that this "Magic" is in full effect and I'm still a student of its inner workings.

Not to say that I have it so down pact that it 100% all the time works but it yields a high enough percentage to make me smile. I'm working on that big bag of money appearing out of thin air, so I can laugh last and the hardest, while shaking my mental fist.

The point being, is whatever you invest your thoughts and energy into, you will get a return on your investment. Invest wisely in the stock market of Life then you will be sure to win big and keep losses to a minimum then things can change like magic or something like it.

Volume I – Chapter 1: The Calling & the Cracks

Section 1: The Divine Pour

Subtitle: When the Cup Overflows, Let It Spill into the World

"The divine doesn't whisper when it moves—it floods."

There comes a moment in your life when the divine doesn't just drip into your consciousness—it pours. It doesn't come politely. It comes with thunder, with clarity, with purpose. That moment for me was not in a church pew or on a meditation cushion. It was in the middle of real life—hair in my hands, doing a client's locs, Alan Watts in my ear, and BOOM: the realization that God wasn't just with me… God was me.

My knees buckled. I had to step outside and catch my breath. The air hit different. The sky looked different. I looked different.

All my life, seeds were being planted—books like 'The Secret,' 'Conversations with God,' 'The Laws of Thinking.' They were truth, but just the tip of the iceberg. Universal laws like gravity—useful, but misunderstood. That day in September 2020, I didn't just understand the message. I *became* it. The veil lifted. The siren sounded. I remembered.

We are not made in God's image just to admire the reflection—we are the reflection. We are the divine, fragmented and refracted into form, here to remember, rewire, and re-create.

Journal Prompt: When was the last time you felt the divine pour into your awareness? What did it feel like in your body?

Affirmation: I am not waiting for the divine—I AM the divine in motion. I remember who I am.

Volume I – Chapter 1: The Calling & the Cracks

Section 2: The Cracks Where the Light Came In

Subtitle: A Sacred Shattering

> "Some of the most beautiful light finds us
> through the cracks we tried to seal shut."

I wasn't born woke. I was born aware—and then gaslit out of it.

Even as a child, I knew things I couldn't explain. I felt things others didn't seem to feel. My dreams were portals, my imagination was sacred technology, and sometimes... the veil between this world and the next felt paper-thin. I didn't always have the words, but the knowing? It was always there.

But life came with its own curriculum. And some of the lessons didn't come easy.

There was trauma. There was favoritism. There were rooms I wasn't safe in. There were feelings I didn't know how to name. There was a storm of survival that I was born into—but even then, a golden thread ran through it all. A knowing that I was meant for something. That all this couldn't be just it.

I saw spirits. I heard voices. I had dreams that would come true. My sister and I once found a "closet portal"—a Narnia-like space where we would visit a strange "friend" who only we could see. And when the portal disappeared years later, I wondered if it was ever real… or if I had just stopped believing.

As I got older, I tried to tuck the magic away. I had to survive in the real world. School. Work. Bills. Family. And yet, the magic never left me. It just whispered beneath the noise. Sometimes it roared through breakdowns and quieted in the middle of doing someone's hair.

I learned how to armor up. But I also learned how to listen. And it was in the listening that the light began to pour through the cracks I used to hide.

I look back now and I understand: the pain wasn't a punishment. It was a pressure. And pressure creates clarity. It squeezes out the lies we've been taught and makes space for the truth to rise.

The cracks didn't break me.

They made room for the light to get in.

And through that light, I remembered: I didn't come here to be perfect. I came here to remember. And in that remembering, I came to heal.

Journal Reflection: Where have the cracks in your life made room for light to enter? What "flaws" or breakdowns actually led you closer to your truth?

Affirmation: My cracks are not my shame. They are sacred spaces where the light of remembrance flows through me.

Volume I – Chapter 1: The Calling & the Cracks

Section 3: The Day Everything Changed

Subtitle: When the Divine Became Literal

> "It didn't whisper. It struck like lightning. And I'll never unknow it again."

September 2020.

I was doing a client's hair, just like any other day, when a lecture by Alan Watts played in the background. I'd heard dozens of his talks before. I'd read The Secret, Conversations with God, The Laws of Thinking. I'd dabbled in universal laws and manifestation. I believed in them the way people believe in gravity—something always in play, but taken for granted.

But that day...

Something clicked.

No—that's not even the right word. It detonated.

I felt my knees go weak. My breath left my body. I had to step outside for air. Not because I was sick—because I had just witnessed something so real, so absolute, it cracked me open..

Not a metaphor. Not a lofty spiritual phrase.

A literal truth.

The divine is not out there, watching from a distance.

It's in here—experiencing life as me. As you.

And in that moment, everything I thought I knew collapsed. And everything I had always felt… was confirmed.

I remembered a talk I had with God when I was eight.

I remembered thinking, "I must have similarities of God—but I'm not God."

But I was wrong.

It wasn't just similarity—it was Source.

We are pieces of God, scattered and tethered. And the whole game is remembering that.

We've been conditioned to create hell with our own thoughts—and call it normal.

To fear our own power and outsource it to systems designed to keep us small.

But once you see the truth, you can't unsee it.

You can't go back to begging when you know you're the source.

It's like God made us in Her image and said,

"I'm gonna make you forget… so when you remember, it'll be the sweetest awakening."

Journal Reflection:

Can you remember a moment when something spiritual became real for you? What did it shift in you?

Affirmation:

I am not just made in God's image—I am God in form, remembering my power with every breath I take.

Volume I – Chapter 1: The Calling & the Cracks

Section 4: From Wishing Wells to Quantum Fields

Subtitle: The Shift from Hoping to Knowing

> "I stopped tossing coins into wishing wells and started commanding waves in quantum fields."

For years, I was a believer.

A hoping believer.

I believed in prayer, in possibility, in the law of attraction. I threw coins into the well, lit candles, made vision boards, and spoke affirmations. And you know what? Some of it worked. Enough to keep the faith alive.

But I didn't know I was still operating like a spiritual beggar.

I was still hoping for things to change, still wishing for the shift—like I was on the outside of Heaven's gate, peeking through the keyhole, waiting for someone to let me in.

A message came, after I heard someone say "God sho' moves in mysterious ways!"

One of the clearest divine downloads I've ever received:

"It's not a mystery. It's math.

I don't move in mysterious ways.

I move in mathematical ones.", almost scoffing when it was said.

Just like gravity, frequency, electromagnetism—there are laws to this thing.

You don't attract what you want.

You attract what you are.

I realized I wasn't waiting on a miracle. The miracle was waiting on me to align with it.

And that's when it hit me: wishing wells are symbolic. You drop something into water, trusting it will ripple. You throw your desire into the unknown, hoping it reaches somewhere sacred.

But now? I understand the field. The frequency. The formula.

Wishing is passive. Commanding is creative.

You don't toss pennies anymore—you send vibrational blueprints.

You don't hope to be chosen—you realize you've already been called.

The quantum field doesn't operate on desperation. It responds to direction.

It mirrors your vibration and multiplies it. Every thought, every feeling, every word—it's coding reality.

And that's the truth so many of us were never told. That we are creators—not just believers. Architects—not just admirers. We're not waiting for God to rescue us from the world. We are God, rescuing OURSELVES by remembering the truth.

The wishing well days are over.

Now we speak, align, move, and receive—on purpose.

Journal Reflection:

Where in your life have you been hoping instead of commanding?

What would shift if you stopped wishing and started aligning?

Affirmation:

I am no longer a hopeful beggar. I am a quantum creator aligned with divine law and infinite possibility.

Volume I – Chapter 1: The Calling & the Cracks

Section 5: How I Know This Is Real

Subtitle: The Receipts from the Realm

> "I don't just believe it. I've lived it. And I have the spiritual scars and miracles to prove it."

This isn't just theory to me. It's not just philosophy or pretty words.

It's not just books I've read or lectures I've listened to.

I know this truth in my bones because life tested me with fire—and the divine showed up inside the flames.

I've been hit by five major car accidents.

Not fender benders—life-altering collisions.

One of them was on the highway, spinning 360's.

One required the jaws of life to get me out.

One left me unable to walk for four months.

Another happened, flipped my vehicle completely, just three months after I lost my sister to cancer—and our family had just buried our brother-in-law, who passed on the same day she was diagnosed.

And still—I am here.

Alive. Breathing. Creating.

That's not coincidence. That's not luck.

That's purpose.

Every time life tried to end me, God reminded me that I was just beginning.

Every time I thought it was over, I was actually being reintroduced to the next version of me.

I've survived trauma that would've broken someone else's mind.

I've lost people I couldn't imagine living without.

I've stood in front of mirrors asking myself if it was all worth it.

And every single time, Spirit said: "Yes. Because your survival is your sermon."

You don't get to this kind of knowing without receipts.

And I've got the emotional x-rays, spiritual bruises, and divine downloads to prove it.

That's why I'm not here to argue with anyone about God.

I've met God. In the hospital bed. In the car wreck. In the midnight cry.

And every single time—it was me that showed up. The divine version of me. The one that can't be killed, silenced, or forgotten.

I'm not telling you this because it sounds good.

I'm telling you because it saved my life.

Journal Reflection:

What life moments have been your spiritual receipts?

Where has your pain confirmed your purpose?

Affirmation:

My story is my testimony. My survival is my spiritual receipt. I am proof that the divine lives within.

Volume I – Chapter 1: The Calling & the Cracks

Section 6: The Flawed Messenger

Subtitle: Why I Was Chosen Anyway

"God didn't pick me because I was perfect. God picked me because I'm real."

You might be wondering:

Why you?

Why me?

Why would a message this sacred come through a vessel like this?

Somebody who's cussed people out, smoked, drank, doubted, and done a whole lot of "unholy" things by society's standards?

Because that's exactly why.

God didn't need a sanitized saint to carry this truth.

God needed someone who had lived in the mud and still bloomed.

Someone who could walk into a church, a trap house, a boardroom, or a barber shop and still carry the same frequency.

I am not perfect. I am a patchwork of holy scars and street-smart wisdom.

I've been the healer and the wounded. The teacher and the student.

I've been curled on the bathroom floor asking if I was crazy for believing any of this—and then turned around and helped someone else awaken the God in them.

I don't fit the mold.

And that's the point.

Because the people who need this message the most?

They don't fit the mold either.

They're the ones who've been told they're too much. Too broken. Too hood. Too loud. Too gay. Too angry. Too sensitive. Too real.

And yet—those are the ones who carry the code.

So no, I don't show up in robes with incense and a halo.

I show up in a hoodie and Timbo's, smoking a fatty, with a journal full of downloads and a heart full of heaven

And I'm not asking for permission anymore. I've made peace with the fact that I won't be accepted by everybody.

But I will be understood by the ones who need to hear me most.

If you've ever felt like you weren't qualified to walk in divine power because of your past or your personality—let me be your proof.

You're not disqualified. You're designed.

God knew exactly what kind of messenger this generation needed.

And sometimes, it's the ones they least expect that carry the loudest truth.

Journal Reflection:

Where have you doubted your worthiness to lead, love, or create because of your flaws?

What if your flaws are actually part of your divine design?

Affirmation:

I am not perfect—but I am powerful. I am a divine messenger, flaws and all, called for this very moment.

God's Got Jokes: Humor as Holy Frequency

"If God didn't have a sense of humor, He wouldn't have sent me."

—Idara Umana

You ever look at your life and laugh so hard it felt like a divine setup? Like the Creator had your name in the writers' room and threw in some plot twists just for comic relief?

That's because God is funny.

Not petty funny—but "I got a point to make" funny.

Spirit doesn't just heal through tears—it heals through laughter. I'm living proof.

If the world expected the Messiah to show up in robes and sandals, I came through wearing gold ropes, lip service, and jokes. A little bit ghetto, a little bit genius. Full of contradictions. And full of God. That's the gag.

This section is your reminder: being Divine doesn't mean being boring.

It means being alive. In color. In rhythm. In full expression.

And yes—sometimes the lesson will come wrapped in sarcasm, meme energy, or a cosmic punchline.

Humor is holy.

It breaks tension.

It opens minds.

It softens trauma.

It sneaks truth past the ego.

God knew exactly what They were doing when They sent me—flaws, fabulousness, and all.

The same way They sent you.

With your quirks. Your gifts. Your awkwardness. Your glow.

So laugh.

Laugh at the illusion.

Laugh at the chaos.

Laugh at the part of you that ever thought you weren't divine enough.

Then wipe your eyes, fix your crown, and go be the miracle you were sent here to be.

Journal Prompt:

What's one moment in your life that felt like divine comedy? What lesson was hidden in the laughter?

Affirmation:

"My joy is my genius. My humor is holy. I am the punchline and the prophecy."

Volume I – Chapter 1: The Calling & the Cracks

Section 7: You Weren't Meant to Read This Until Now

Subtitle: The Divine Timing of Your Awakening

> "You didn't find this book. It found the version of you who could finally receive it."

You weren't meant to read this before now.

Not because you weren't ready back then—but because the you that's reading this today?

This is the version who can interpret it.

Hold it.

Use it.

Every step you've taken, every twist and wound and wonder—it's all led you here.

Right here.

Reading these words with a heart that remembers, even if your mind still doubts.

You didn't miss your moment.

You became your moment.

That's how divine timing works.

It doesn't operate on clocks. It operates on readiness.

See, truth is vibrational. It's coded.

It waits in books, in people, in messages—until your soul is tuned to the right frequency to hear it.

And baby, you're tuned in.

That's why this doesn't feel like new information.

It feels like remembering.

You're not crazy for feeling like everything is accelerating.

You're not delusional for seeing signs everywhere.

You're not imagining it—your soul is waking up, and the Universe is responding.

This book isn't just a book. It's a mirror. A map. A matchstick. A magnet.

It's been waiting on you, the you who's been cracked open just enough to let the light in, and the truth back out.

So no, this isn't coincidence. This is coincide(nce). A co-incident. Incidents that are partners. Even the sound of the word phonetically is INSIDE. .

A divine collision.

And I promise you—if you lean in, if you stay with it—this won't just be something you read.

It'll be something you become.

Journal Reflection:

What had to happen for you to arrive at this moment of readiness?

What parts of you are waking up right now?

Affirmation:

I am not behind. I am not lost. I arrived right on time, and I am ready to receive what is mine.

God Intentions

Poem

The road to hell is paved with good intentions, so I must make my soul safe.

My time, love or talent won't wait or waste.

I know squandering them will make them waste away.

Can't replace the irreplaceable.

While I have air in my lungs and a thought in my brain means I'm fully capable.

I promise to achieve, 'til I reach the inner depths of me, turn it into energy, and fuel my drive.

Electrify my soul until I feel alive!! Til I've created a monster, worse than Frankenstein, when it comes to makin' mine and getting it in.

Don't play the game unless you came to WIN!

There's too many people standing in the stands, stuck in the standstill of life, cheering on the movers and shakers of Action.

Looking at what you want, who you are and what you're becoming is a stand-off and you can't get no satisfaction.. life ain't no dress rehearsal, there is no practicing.

And everything happens for a reason, there are no accidents.

So I have a purpose why I was put here, and it damn sure wasn't just to cheer.

And not taking nothing away from cheerleaders cuz at times I do it.

But my dream is NOT that and it WILL be manifested to prove it.

It's been too many people, cold in the grave, buried with good intentions, well wishes, hopes, dreams and more in store.

That made stepping stones permanent places, sad in their core

And I know they had every intention of making it all come true, like we all do.

Or even worse the ones that are here and not living their life out loud and not their truth.

So busy with their heads in strange clouds and earthly things, to be your own captain..

10 years later they look back like "What happened?

Time sure does fly fast, I looked down and it just passed my ass."

Only a fool squanders valuables and I will hold myself accountable for being foolish.

I hold the gold and make all of the rules with.

I've taken for granted time, love and talent, I couldn't imagine if they left me empty when there was plenty.

I'm on the elevator of me and I'm going to the next level and I encourage anyone to do the same or you be meeting the devil on that road paved to Hell, catching wishes.

Tarred and scarred with your good intentions...

December 15, 2013 I read this poem exactly 5 years later on the day of opening my boutique Gold Star Gallery

Volume I - Chapter 2: Personal Revelations & Divine Downloads

---

Volume I – Chapter 2: Personal Revelations & Divine Downloads

Section 1: A Lifetime of Seeds

Subtitle: How My Journey Was Prepared Long Before I Knew I Was Walking It

> "The path wasn't revealed to me all at once. It was whispered—seed by seed, until I bloomed."

Looking back now, I see it clearly: the divine had been speaking to me my whole life.

But I didn't always recognize the voice.

Sometimes it came through books. Sometimes dreams.

Other times, it was through pain, signs, symbols, whispers, and wonders that didn't make sense... until they did.

Truth wasn't something I stumbled on by accident.

It was planted in me—on purpose.

And even when I didn't water it with belief or understanding, it grew anyway.

I remember reading books like The Secret,
Conversations with God, and The Laws of Thinking.

Each one left an imprint. Not because I fully grasped
it at the time, but because it was unlocking a part of
me that already knew.

The idea that we create our reality? That thoughts
carry weight? That God is not separate, but within?

These were not new ideas. They were buried codes in
my spirit waiting to be reactivated.

I didn't know it then, but those tiny awakenings were
breadcrumbs.

Seeds of remembrance placed just far enough apart
that I'd have to journey inward to find them all.

Even my childhood was laced with signs:

Dreams that felt more like visitations and even came
true.

A mysterious portal in a closet where my sister and I
used to "go visit our friend."

Out-of-body experiences.

A deep knowing that I was never just human. But like
many of us, I brushed it off.

Life got louder. Trauma got heavier. Survival mode set
in.

And those seeds? They waited. Until the right
moment.

Until the day came when the ground cracked, the light got in, and the roots of everything I had ever doubted reached upward and whispered:

"Now. Grow."

Journal Reflection: What spiritual "seeds" were planted in your past that make more sense now? What truths have been growing quietly in you?

Affirmation: Every experience was a seed of remembrance. I trust the divine timing of my bloom.

Volume I – Chapter 2: Personal Revelations & Divine Downloads

Section 2: The Closet Portal and Childhood Signs

Subtitle: The Sacred Strange That Was Always Guiding Me

> "I thought I had an overactive imagination.
> Turns out, I had an under-acknowledged gift."

Before I ever had the language to describe it, I knew this world wasn't all there was.

As a child, I saw what others didn't. Felt what others dismissed.

And while some chalked it up to childhood imagination, I now know—my spirit was wide open.

One of the clearest signs came in the most unexpected place:

a stairwell closet.

My sister and I used to enter that makeshift closet, which was placed between the stairwell of our 2-family flat, and "go visit our friend."

We didn't question it. It felt normal to us—like walking into another realm was just part of playtime.

We'd close the door within the wall, step inside the dark, and somehow… end up somewhere else.

Time would pass strangely. It wasn't scary—it was comforting. Like visiting a place that knew us.

We didn't have to explain anything. We belonged there.

And then one day, after we hadn't visited in a while for playtime, the portal was just… gone.

We tried to go back, but it didn't work anymore. I think we got occupied with life and our innocence lost.

The doorway had closed.

And it left a quiet ache in us that we couldn't name.

But now I understand: that portal was real.

It was spiritual technology cloaked in simplicity— proof that children are tuned into frequencies adults forget how to hear.

And that wasn't the only sign.

I had prophetic dreams.

Out-of-body experiences.

I could feel energy so deeply that sometimes it overwhelmed me.

I was picking up on thoughts, emotions, and vibrations like an antenna—but I had no manual for what I was receiving.

There were moments I'd wake up crying without knowing why, or feel other people's emotions as if they were mine.

I wasn't "too sensitive." I was spiritually attuned.

But because the world didn't validate it, I learned to doubt myself.

To suppress the magic.

In my heart of knowing, I normalized the supernatural.

Only now do I realize: those early signs were my spiritual resume.

A divine record that I was always chosen, always connected, and always being prepared.

What I once thought was odd, I now recognize as origin.

And the portal? It never left. It just moved inside me.

Journal Reflection:

What spiritual experiences did you have as a child that you later dismissed?

How might they have been signs of your divine sensitivity?

Affirmation:

I reclaim the sacred signs of my childhood. My gifts were real, and they are returning stronger than ever.

Volume I – Chapter 2: Personal Revelations & Divine Downloads

Section 3: I Don't Move in Mysterious Ways—It's Math

Subtitle: The Sacred Code Hidden in Plain Sight

> "It's not a MYSTERY. It's MATH. I don't move in mysterious ways—I move in mathematical ones." —God

---

That message hit me like a lightning bolt from the soul.

I remember it clearly.

A divine download. A voice—not external, but internal—calm, firm, and undeniable.

And it said:

"I don't move in mysterious ways. I move in mathematical ones."

That was the moment it all began to click:

Manifestation isn't random.

Spiritual power isn't mysterious.

Miracles aren't magic tricks.

It's patterns.

It's formulas.

It's sacred geometry.

It's divine equation.

God doesn't roll dice in the sky.

God sets laws in motion—unchanging, constant, like gravity for the spirit.

And that's why so many of us have suffered—not because we're cursed or forgotten, but because we weren't taught the math.

We were taught to pray, to beg, to plead for a rescue…

but never taught how to calculate the energy we were radiating or attracting.

It's like being handed a checkbook with infinite money but no one told you how to sign your name.

You've got the power—but not the programming.

That's what this realization shattered open for me:

The "mystery" of God is actually divine science.

A language of numbers, vibration, geometry, energy, and emotion.

Emotion + Intention = Vibration

Vibration + Duration = Manifestation

Manifestation + Alignment = Miracles

That's not superstition. That's sacred circuitry.

It's divine mathematics.

A God Code written into the fabric of the Universe—
and the blueprint of your being.

So no, it's not mysterious why things fall apart when
you're stuck in fear.

It's not mysterious why blessings follow gratitude, or
why pain multiplies when you rehearse it.

It's math.

And when you learn the formula, you stop waiting for
miracles to fall from the sky…

and start co-creating them right here on Earth.

Universal Law:

Law of Cause and Effect — Every action (seen or
unseen) has a corresponding reaction. Nothing
happens by chance. The spiritual field is governed by
energetic cause and measurable effect.

Scientific Insight:

The Law of Vibration underpins all physical reality. Everything—sound, light, matter—is made of energy oscillating at specific frequencies. Even thoughts emit measurable electromagnetic waves.

Journal Reflection:

What outcomes in your life could be traced back to unconscious "equations" you've been running?

What new formula would you like to start using—on purpose?

Affirmation:

The divine is not distant or chaotic—it is precise, ordered, and intelligent. I align with the sacred code. I learn the math. I move with the field.

Volume I – Chapter 2: Personal Revelations & Divine Downloads

Section 4: God Is Not Separate—God Is the Source Within

Subtitle: The Return to Divine Identity

> "You were never disconnected from God. You were just distracted from the connection."

For most of my life, I was taught that God was far away.

Somewhere in the sky. Up above. Out there.

Watching. Judging. Waiting for me to get it right.

And because of that belief, I prayed like a beggar.

I doubted myself constantly.

I lived with the unspoken ache that something greater might one day save me—if I was good enough.

But then something sacred shattered that illusion.

It didn't come through a preacher.

It came through presence. Through stillness.

Through the unraveling of what I thought was truth.

And the revelation came in clear, unshakable clarity:

God is not separate. God is the Source within.

Not in a poetic, symbolic way.

But in a literal, electrical, energetic, living way.

That power I was always reaching for?

I was reaching from it.

That love I kept seeking in other people?

It had been flowing through me the whole time.

That guidance I begged for in the dark?

It had always been my intuition whispering with divine rhythm.

When I finally accepted this truth, something inside me rearranged.

It wasn't that I became divine.

It was that I remembered I already was.

I stopped seeing myself as a tiny speck beneath the heavens…

and started recognizing myself as a sacred spark of the heavens.

I'm not an orphan hoping for God's approval.

I'm God's expression—breathing, thinking, creating, laughing, healing, evolving, and sometimes falling apart just to become something even more beautiful.

And so are you.

We are all divine sparks in disguise.

We were just taught to forget it.

But here's the beautiful part:

The moment you stop searching for God outside yourself is the moment you remember the truth inside yourself.

Universal Law:

Law of Divine Oneness — Everything in the Universe is interconnected. There is no separation between you and Source. Every thought, action, and energy you emit ripples into the whole.

Scientific Insight:

Quantum physics shows that at the subatomic level, all things are entangled. The observer affects the observed. Consciousness doesn't just witness reality— it shapes it. You aren't separate from the Universe; you are the Universe expressing itself uniquely.

Journal Reflection: Where in your life have you been searching for God outside of yourself?

How does it feel to reclaim that sacred source within?

Affirmation: I am not separate from the Divine. I am the Divine expressed in human form. The power I seek is the power I am.

Volume I – Chapter 2: Personal Revelations & Divine Downloads

Section 5: The Epiphany at Age 8

Subtitle: The First Time God Told Me Who I Was

> "I didn't fully understand what I was feeling back then, but now I know: God was already whispering the blueprint to me."

I was just eight years old.

A child with big eyes, a sensitive heart, and an inner knowing I couldn't explain.

And somewhere in the quiet of that age—before the world got too loud, before people taught me to doubt—I had one of many talks with God.

Not with a booming voice from the sky, but with the presence I felt inside me.

There was no ceremony. No church pew. No theology.

I used to go to a Catholic grade school and I always had a lot of questions because of what I personally experienced and what they said I "should" experience.

They always said we are God's children, then one day God said "So do you think your earthly parents passed down some things to you?"

And I thought about it and said "They say I look like my Mom".

Me, always such a literal person and especially being a child, I only thought God was referring to the surface.

Then God said "You are able to do things like your mother and father can do, right?"

I said yes again then God said "Since you are a child of God, do you think you can do things I can do?"

And I didn't know what to think but it planted a seed within me.

Just me and the voice of the Universe wrapped around my spirit like warm wind.

And what I heard was simple, yet infinite:

"You are a creator too." God said.

I didn't even know how to fully process it.

But I remember the feeling.

Like electricity and peace mixed together.

Like someone had handed me a key to something I didn't know was locked.

At that age, I didn't have the words to explain it to anyone.

So I tucked it away.

I went on being a child, moving through life, collecting experiences and stories and scars.

But the memory never left me.

And as I grew, the truth began to circle back.

That moment became a thread I could trace through everything.

Through the books I was drawn to.

Through the dreams and the signs and the moments I thought were just "coincidence."

And later—decades later—when my knees buckled during that Alan Watts lecture in 2020, I remembered.

I remembered that eight-year-old girl who already knew she was a piece of God.

A co-creator.

A mirror of the divine.

And it broke me wide open.

Because the truth isn't something we learn.

It's something we remember.

Universal Law:

Law of Correspondence — As above, so below. As within, so without. The divine truth you carry is reflected in your inner and outer reality—no matter your age or awareness.

Scientific Insight:

Studies on childhood cognition and spiritual development show that children often access heightened states of awareness, creative imagination, and intuitive intelligence before being conditioned out of it. What we call "pretend" is often perception unfiltered.

Journal Reflection:

Can you remember a moment from your childhood where you felt especially connected, powerful, or aware of something "bigger"? What did that version of you know that you've forgotten?

Affirmation:

The divine truth has always been with me. I honor the child in me who heard it first, and I let her wisdom rise again.

Volume I – Chapter 2: Personal Revelations & Divine Downloads

Section 6: If You Feed Them, You Will Never Go Hungry

Subtitle: The Divine Law of Sacred Reciprocity

> "If you feed them, you will never go hungry." — God

This wasn't a metaphor.

It was a message.

A divine whisper I heard during one of the most intense seasons of my life.

I thought it was about food. About service. About making sure others were full.

But over time, I realized—this was spiritual law disguised as a sentence.

It was God explaining the Law of Circulation in a language I could feel.

Because what you give from the soul—whether it's nourishment, wisdom, art, love, laughter, or light—will come back to you multiplied.

Not always from the same source.

But always from the same field.

And when I looked back, I saw it had always been true.

When I gave love, even when I was empty, I still received support.

When I poured into others—even without knowing how I'd refill—I somehow stayed full.

Every time I showed up with open hands and open heart, the Universe matched me.

At first, I thought this download was about my restaurant, or feeding people in the literal sense.

And yes—it did show up that way too.

But the deeper truth?

It was about this—the book, the message, the movement.

It was about the spiritual food.

The ideas that nourish souls.

The stories that remind people of who they are.

The energy that wakes up someone's inner giant and says, Eat. Rise. Remember.

That's what I'm here to serve.

And I trust now, without question:

If I feed the people truth, I will never lack what I need.

Universal Law:

Law of Compensation — The Universe returns to you what you give in energy, effort, love, and faith. Every act of generosity, no matter how small, creates a ripple that echoes back in divine timing.

Scientific Insight:

Studies in neurobiology show that acts of service release serotonin, dopamine, and oxytocin—the brain's "fulfillment cocktail" creates a "helper's high"—proving that giving literally nourishes your body, mind, and spirit.

Journal Reflection:

What do you have inside of you that nourishes others? How have you seen your giving come back to you—spiritually, emotionally, or even materially?

Affirmation:

As I pour into others, I am divinely poured into. I feed with love and am never left hungry.

Volume I – Chapter 2: Personal Revelations & Divine Downloads

Section 7: The Hair Chair and the Sacred Downloads

Subtitle: Where Spirit Spoke While I Styled

> "Some people channel in caves. I channeled in hair, locs and coils."

My salon chair was never just a place for beauty—it was a portal.

People came for their hair, but they left with healing.

Because while I was parting hair, Spirit was parting veils.

While I was twisting roots, downloads were locked into me.

The hum of the blow dryer became background music to divine truth whispering in my ear.

Sometimes I'd be mid-retwist or scalp massage, and the deepest epiphany would rise up from nowhere— like it had been waiting for me to be still and in flow.

And I realized:

That chair was my altar.

My hands were anointed.

The conversations were confessions, prophecies, breakthroughs.

People cried.

People laughed.

People heard themselves clearly for the first time in years.

And I did too.

That chair taught me that everyday life is holy ground.

That sacred downloads don't always need incense and chants.

Sometimes they show up in the smell of Joyberry Oil or Apple Cider Vinegar.

That's how Spirit works—not just through meditation and stillness, but through movement, service, and skill.

So I started honoring that space.

Every client was a divine appointment.

Every appointment was a classroom.

And every download? A building block in this book.

Universal Law:

Law of Divine Purpose — Your gifts and environments are not random. They are tools and classrooms for sacred evolution and revelation.

Scientific Insight:

Entering a state of "flow" (as in hairstyling or focused creativity) triggers theta brain waves—the same frequency found in deep meditation and trance states, where intuition and downloads flourish.

Journal Reflection:

Where in your everyday life does Spirit speak to you most clearly? What "ordinary" space has become sacred for you?

Affirmation:

My gifts are portals. My workspace is holy ground. Spirit flows through my hands and fills the room with truth.

Volume I – Chapter 2: Personal Revelations & Divine Downloads

Section 8: The Moment I Remembered Where God Is

Subtitle: The Download That Shattered the Lie of Separation

> "I thought it was just a metaphor… until it dropped me to my knees."

It was September 2020.

My knees buckled.

I had to step outside for air.

It felt like lightning and peace at the same time.

Because in that moment, I didn't just think the idea.

I knew—without question—that I am GOD in the flesh.

Not in the blasphemous way they warned us about.

Not in arrogance.

But in recognition.

I remembered every experience, right place moments, and breadcrumbs.

And it all came full circle:

I am not just made in God's image.

I am an extension. A reflection. A frequency of the Infinite.

I felt empowered —and tricked.

Because I realized: we've been taught to forget. On purpose.

When I say I felt betrayed and liberated at the same time, I mean it. It felt like I'd been tricked out of my own power… only to discover it had been mine the whole time.

And suddenly, I thought of all the times I prayed in fear, cried in desperation until my eyes swell shut, begging for miracles —when the miracle was already me.

We've been taught to worship outside of ourselves, to fear our own power, to attribute our miracles to something distant…

When we've been the miracle machines the whole time.

I remember in my early teen's, God whispered in my ear "What good is a God that doesn't know they are God?". The magnitude of that statement became overstood that day.

This is the Good News.

Not just that God is real.

But that God is here. Inside. Awake. Creative. Ready.

We are creators too.

And the lie that kept us from knowing that?

It's the biggest spiritual robbery of all time.

Universal Law:

Law of Identity — What you recognize as true becomes your lived experience. When you know you are divine, you begin to live in divine alignment and authority.

Scientific Insight:

Mirror neurons and self-perception studies show that identity isn't fixed—it's programmable. When you embody a new truth (especially one aligned with empowerment), your brain rewires itself to match it.

Journal Reflection:

What were you taught to believe about your connection to God? What feels different now that you've remembered your divinity?

Affirmation:

I am not separate from Source. I am the Source remembered, embodied, and expressed.

Volume I – Chapter 2: Personal Revelations & Divine Downloads

Section 9: The Master Mechanic Analogy

Subtitle: God Didn't Just Build the Car—God Became the Driver

> "When a master mechanic builds their dream car, do you think they just park it in the garage?"

This download came through like divine analogy wrapped in motor oil and cosmic insight.

Imagine this:

A master mechanic designs the perfect ride—every part precision-tuned, every system flowing in harmony. It's the car of their dreams. The one they poured all their brilliance, time, and love into. The kind that turns heads and breaks limits.

You think they're just gonna let it sit?

No.

They're going to drive it.

Cruise in it. Style and profile in it.

Push the pedal. Feel the road. Experience the thrill of what they created.

That's what God did with us.

God didn't just create us—God stepped into us.

To move. To feel. To laugh. To cry.

To experience every flavor of existence—sweet, bitter, blazing, and beautiful.

And not just once.

Through every single one of us.

We are divine vehicles—each uniquely built to carry Source through this human experience.

And just like that master mechanic, God made us not just for design… but for expression.

We are vessels of infinite horsepower.

But we keep driving like we're stuck in first gear.

Why? Because we forgot who built us. And what's under the hood.

But once you remember?

You stop asking for rides.

You grab the keys.

And you drive like divinity on a mission.

Universal Law:

Law of Expression — The Creator experiences life through the creation. You are not separate from the masterpiece—you are the masterpiece, animated by the mind that made it.

Scientific Insight:

Neuroscience confirms that embodiment and visualization activate the same neural pathways as the real experience. Believing you are powerful begins activating your actual capacity to perform and transform.

Journal Reflection:

If you're a divine vehicle—how are you driving right now? Are you coasting in fear or shifting into bold creation?

Affirmation:

I am the living vehicle of the Divine. I shift into power, I accelerate in faith, and I drive in purpose.

Volume I – Chapter 2: Personal Revelations & Divine Downloads

Section 10: The Magic Jewelry That We Forgot Was Real

Subtitle: How They Convinced Us to Wear Our Power Like It Was Costume

> "We thought it was just decoration... but it was divine technology all along."

Imagine someone gives you a radiant piece of jewelry.

It's heavy with stones, glowing with mystery. They say,

"It's magic. It regenerates itself. It's yours—use it however you wish."

But it seems too good to be true.

So you smile, say thanks, and wear it for the way it looks... never for what it does.

You forget. Or worse, someone tells you:

"It's fake."

And so for years, you wear it like costume jewelry.

As fashion. As an accessory.

Not realizing it's a billion-dollar artifact of functional spiritual technology.

Until one day—someone who remembers tells you what it really is.

And everything changes.

That's what happened to us.

We were born with divine power. Intuition. Manifestation. Frequency. Command.

We were handed the keys to the kingdom—then taught to keep them in our pocket.

Taught that miracles only happen to the holiest.

That power lives outside of us.

That energy tools like crystals, prayer, sound, and sacred ritual were just decoration—or worse, evil.

And yet every ancient civilization—Egyptian, Mayan, Indigenous, Indian, Kemetic—knew better.

They used crystals, metals, words, symbols, water, geometry, sound, and breath as literal technology.

And now we're remembering.

We're waking up to the truth:

We were never ordinary.

We were just convinced our magic was costume.

But it's real. And it's ours.

Universal Law:

Law of Divine Inheritance — You came into this life equipped with everything you need to thrive, evolve, and manifest. Your power was never outside of you— it was only waiting to be remembered.

Scientific Insight:

Crystals store and transmit energy (like quartz in watches). Frequency and sound (like tuning forks) have been proven to shift human brain states. What once seemed "woo-woo" is now measurable science.

Journal Reflection:

What gifts or tools have you dismissed or ignored because someone told you they weren't "real"? What power are you ready to reclaim?

Affirmation:

My power is not pretend. I remember what they made me forget. I wear my sacred tools as technology, not just decoration.

Volume I – Chapter 2: Personal Revelations & Divine Downloads

Section 11: This Message Was Hidden for You

Subtitle: The Frequency of Readiness Unlocks Revelation

> "This wasn't hidden from you. It was hidden for you—until you became the version of you who could interpret it."

You weren't late.

You weren't slow.

You didn't miss anything.

You simply hadn't become the version of yourself who could understand this level of truth... yet.

That's the thing about divine messages.

They're encoded in a frequency that requires alignment to unlock.

You have to vibrate at the level of the lesson in order to even hear it correctly.

Some messages won't make sense until your heart softens.

Until your ego quiets.

Until your trauma clears just enough to let the light in.

That's why you could read the same book ten years apart and have two completely different revelations.

Not because the book changed—but because you did.

So if you're reading this now, it's not a coincidence.

It's not random.

It's not just a "good time" in your life.

It's divine alignment.

The teacher appears when the student is ready.

The code unlocks when the keyholder arrives.

The frequency matches, and boom—the veil lifts.

You weren't meant to read this until now.

Because now… you're ready.

Universal Law:

Law of Correspondence — As within, so without. As your internal reality shifts, your outer world delivers new reflections—books, people, messages—that match your new vibration.

Scientific Insight:

Cognitive resonance research shows we literally cannot perceive or retain information that's out of alignment with our current beliefs or identity. Once we shift, new meaning appears in old things.

Journal Reflection:

What wisdom are you finally able to receive now that you couldn't before? What version of yourself had to arrive in order to "get it"?

Affirmation:

I receive the messages meant for me in divine timing. I'm vibrating at the level of revelation.

Volume I – Chapter 2: Personal Revelations & Divine Downloads

Section 12: Divine Timing Is a Strategy, Not a Delay

Subtitle: The Universe Isn't Slow—It's Calculated

"God's not stalling. God is sequencing."

We love to say "everything happens for a reason,"

but the deeper truth?

Everything happens by design.

We think we're waiting on the blessing,

but really, the blessing is waiting on us.

Waiting on our maturity.

Our healed mind.

Our bold YES!!

Our spiritual passwords to activate what's already been built in another dimension.

Because divine timing isn't about making you wait.

It's about making sure you can hold what's coming without fumbling it.

And when it finally comes?

You'll realize it wasn't a delay.

It was a perfect orchestration.

The people you had to meet.

The detours that humbled you.

The heartbreak that cleared your lens.

The breakdown that turned into a launch pad.

You couldn't have handled this version of the blessing in a past version of you.

It had to marinate.

Just like seeds underground—germinating in the dark, not forgotten.

Universal Law:

Law of Gestation — Every creation has an incubation period. Just as a baby takes time to form in the womb, your manifestations need time to develop and align with your readiness.

Scientific Insight:

Quantum physics shows that multiple outcomes exist in potential until observed or interacted with. Delayed outcomes are often the result of complexity and interconnected alignment—not denial.

Journal Reflection:

Where in your life have you seen divine timing work in your favor, even if it didn't feel like it at first?

Affirmation:

I trust the divine sequence of my life. What's meant for me is forming in precision and power.

Volume I – Chapter 2: Personal Revelations & Divine Downloads

Section 13: The Grand Scheme of "Me"

Subtitle: Nothing Was Wasted, Not Even the Wreckage

"It wasn't random. It was refining."

Every single experience.

Every wound.

Every joy.

Every loss.

Every delay.

Every divine detour...

It was all shaping me. Preparing me.

Turning me into the vessel that could hold this truth and carry this message.

When people say, "Trust the process,"

I say—No. TRUST YOURSELF inside the process.

Because what looked like chaos was really choreography.

It wasn't just the grand scheme of things.

It was the Grand Scheme of Me.

Of course I didn't understand it while I was in it.

Of course it felt cruel and confusing sometimes.

But now?

I see it.

That heartbreak taught me discernment.

That betrayal sharpened my spiritual boundaries.

That loss expanded my compassion.

That rock bottom rerouted me toward my real power.

Nothing was wasted.

Not even the things that nearly broke me.

Especially not those.

Because I needed to die in the cocoon before I could resurrect with wings.

Universal Law:

Law of Polarity — Every experience contains its opposite. Within every hardship lies the seed of its opposite blessing, wisdom, or breakthrough.

Scientific Insight:

Neuroplasticity proves the brain can rewire itself after trauma—adversity literally shapes new growth, empathy, and resilience when met with awareness and intention.

Journal Reflection: What painful or confusing moments now make sense in hindsight? What might have actually been a spiritual setup?

Affirmation: Every piece of my journey has purpose. My path was never punishment—it was preparation.

Volume I – Chapter 2: Personal Revelations & Divine Downloads

Section 14: Every Breadcrumb Led Here

Subtitle: The Trail Wasn't Random. It Was Coded.

> "The signs were always there. I just didn't know they were signs yet."

Looking back now, I see it.

The breadcrumbs.

The clues.

The divine nudges that I mistook for coincidences.

They were everywhere.

The dreams I used to have.

The books that fell into my hands at just the right time.

The strangers who said things they didn't even realize were answers to questions I hadn't asked out loud.

It was a trail.

A spiritual GPS.

God leading me back to myself.

And sure—I strayed.

I got distracted. I took detours. I fell into pits and patterns.

But every breadcrumb was still there.

Waiting for me to look down and notice.

That's the power of alignment:

You don't have to see the whole path.

Just recognize the breadcrumb in front of you.

And once you start following them with trust?

They multiply.

Because the Universe speaks in whispers.

In patterns.

In synchronicities.

And in hindsight that suddenly makes perfect sense.

Universal Law:

Law of Divine Order — Everything unfolds according to an intelligent and purposeful design, even when it seems chaotic. There are no coincidences—only coded connections.

Scientific Insight:

The Reticular Activating System (RAS) in the brain filters stimuli based on what we deem important. Once you become spiritually aware, your RAS begins flagging divine breadcrumbs more clearly.

Journal Reflection:

What divine breadcrumbs were placed in your life long before you even realized they were leading somewhere?

Affirmation:

The signs were always there. I am now aware enough to follow them with trust and clarity.

Volume I – Chapter 2: Personal Revelations & Divine Downloads

Section 15: The Sacred Setup of My Struggles

Subtitle: I Wasn't Being Punished—Just Positioned

> "If I told you the pain was part of the prophecy, would you still curse it?"

There were moments in my life when I truly thought I was being punished.

Back-to-back betrayals.

Financial droughts.

Near-death experiences.

Unseen tears behind closed doors.

But every time I broke—

I cracked open wider.

Every time I lost—

I released what wasn't mine.

Every time I stumbled—

I slowed down just enough to listen.

What I thought was breaking me…

was actually building me.

It was sacred. It was setup.

It was preparation in disguise.

Because you don't get forged in feathers.

You get forged in fire.

You don't become a diamond through praise.

You become one through pressure.

And God didn't want to punish me.

God wanted to position me.

So when the time came, I wouldn't just carry the message—I'd embody it.

And that's exactly what I'm doing now.

I'm not just telling you how to rise.

I'm showing you that I did.

Universal Law:

Law of Transmutation — Energy can't be destroyed, only transformed. Pain is energy. So is fear. But so is healing, love, and purpose. Everything you've been through is recyclable into power.

Scientific Insight:

Post-traumatic growth is a documented phenomenon where individuals experience greater purpose, strength, and clarity after enduring trauma, especially when they find meaning in the suffering.

Journal Reflection: What struggle in your life actually shaped your strength, voice, or wisdom? Can you reframe it as sacred setup?

Affirmation: My struggles were not setbacks. They were spiritual setups for my greatness.

Volume I – Chapter 2: Personal Revelations & Divine Downloads

Section 16: I Don't Believe in Coincidence— Only Co-Incidence

Subtitle: Everything Aligns in Divine Symphony

> "What they call coincidence, I call choreography."

Coincidence makes it sound accidental.

Like life is rolling dice in the dark.

But I've seen too much magic to believe that anymore.

When the same number shows up on a receipt and on a license plate and in your dream—

That's not random.

When you run into someone from years ago and they say exactly what your spirit needed to hear—

That's not a fluke.

That's co-incidence.

Not as in "oops," but as in two frequencies colliding in divine time.

It's the universe winking at you.

God leaving breadcrumbs.

The matrix bending itself to reflect your awakening.

Everything is connected.

Everything is coded.

It doesn't mean life is always easy—

But it is always meaningful.

And once you start seeing the patterns,

you don't question them anymore.

You follow them.

Like constellations.

Like stars on a map leading you home.

Universal Law:

Law of Vibration — Everything is energy, and similar energies attract one another. What seems like coincidence is actually resonance. You're meeting frequencies that match your own.

Scientific Insight:

Studies in quantum entanglement show particles can be interconnected across distance. Similarly, human consciousness may interact with information fields in ways that defy linear logic.

Journal Reflection:

Think of three moments in your life that seemed too perfectly timed to be random. What might they have been pointing you toward?

Affirmation:

Nothing in my life is random. I walk in co-incidence, not coincidence. My path is coded with purpose.

Volume I – Chapter 2: Personal Revelations & Divine Downloads

Section 17: The Portal Was Never Outside—It Was Me

Subtitle: The Way In Is the Way Through

> "I kept looking for the doorway... until I realized I was the door."

For most of my life, I thought the magic was out there.

In books.

In rituals.

In churches.

In gurus and sacred places.

I searched for the portal.

The "thing" that would crack the code and launch me into full alignment.

But then I realized:

I've always been the portal.

The power didn't live in the candles.

It lived in my intention.

The magic wasn't in the object.

It was in my vibration.

Every breath I took was a key.

Every thought was a spell.

Every heartbeat was a drum calling God back home to me.

I wasn't supposed to find the portal.

I was supposed to remember I AM it.

That's why it never worked trying to chase awakening through someone else's map.

My design is divine and specific.

And so is yours.

You are the bridge.

The path.

The spell.

The sanctuary.

The world within you is the access point to all realms.

Universal Law:

Law of Mentalism — All is mind. The universe is mental. The source of all reality begins in consciousness, meaning the portal to creation begins within.

Scientific Insight:

The placebo effect and quantum observer effect show how belief and attention literally alter outcomes. Consciousness is not passive—it's a powerful generator of experience.

Journal Reflection:

In what ways have you been seeking externally for things that might actually exist within you?

Affirmation:

I am the portal. The sacred doorway to my highest reality lives inside of me.

Volume I – Chapter 2: Personal Revelations & Divine Downloads

Section 18: You're Not Crazy. You're Becoming

Subtitle: Awakening Feels Like Madness Until It Feels Like Freedom

"It's not insanity. It's initiation."

If no one warned you that awakening feels like being cracked open with no anesthesia—

let this be that warning.

It's disorienting at first.

You start seeing through the illusions.

The systems.

The programming.

And suddenly the world you trusted feels… fake.

You cry more.

You isolate more.

You question everything.

And the people around you?

They might say you're changing too fast.

That you've lost it.

That you're not making sense anymore.

But what if the nonsense you're shedding

was never yours to carry?

You're not crazy.

You're becoming.

Becoming more of your true self and less of your conditioned self.

Becoming the version of you that knows, deeply, this ain't all there is.

You were never meant to fit in.

You were meant to remember.

So when it gets messy and loud inside your head—

Pause.

That's your soul reconfiguring its signal.

That's your spirit updating its software.

You're not malfunctioning.

You're upgrading.

Universal Law:

Law of Rhythm — All things rise and fall. Life moves in cycles. Awakening has rhythms: unraveling, remembering, rebuilding. Each phase is essential for alignment.

Scientific Insight:

Neurological rewiring during periods of intense insight or trauma can cause temporary instability—similar to a system update. But post-transition, clarity and coherence improve dramatically.

Journal Reflection:

What part of your "becoming" felt the most misunderstood? Who might you need to forgive—for judging your growth, or for not understanding it?

Affirmation:

I am not broken—I am breaking through. My becoming is holy.

Volume I – Chapter 2: Personal Revelations & Divine Downloads

Section 19: Becoming Is a Divine Side Effect of Remembering

Subtitle: Growth Isn't a Glitch—It's a God-Code Activation

> "Once you remember who you are, you can't stay who you were."

There's a divine side effect to remembering your power:

You start evolving at warp speed.

Old things fall off.

Old friendships feel misaligned.

Old jobs, old habits, old conversations suddenly sound like static.

It's not that you're better than anyone—

it's that you're different now.

You're operating on a new frequency,

and everything that doesn't match it begins to fade like background noise.

And that's not a glitch.

That's God-code activating.

You weren't meant to remember and stay the same.

You were meant to remember and become.

Because remembering who you are sets off a domino effect—

Your posture changes.

Your voice gets clearer.

Your boundaries sharpen.

Your desires become sacred.

And the things that once satisfied you no longer do.

Not because they're bad,

but because you've grown beyond them.

It's like tasting real fruit for the first time after years of candy.

There's no comparison.

You're hungry for something real now.

And you are becoming real.

The more you remember,

the more your becoming becomes undeniable.

Universal Law:

Law of Evolution — Everything in the universe is designed to grow and evolve. Awakening isn't static— it's a living process of becoming more aligned with your divine design.

Scientific Insight:

Neuroscience confirms that as we develop new neural pathways, old habits and preferences weaken. Identity is not fixed—it evolves as consciousness expands.

Journal Reflection:

What parts of your life feel like they no longer resonate with the version of you who's awakening? How can you honor the shift with grace?

Affirmation:

I am becoming who I was born to remember. Growth is sacred, and I welcome my evolution.

Volume I – Chapter 2: Personal Revelations & Divine Downloads

Section 20: This Chapter of You Was Always Meant to Be Written

Subtitle: You Are the Story, the Scribe, and the Sacred Scroll

> "The pen was never in someone else's hand—it's always been yours."

This part of you?

The version reading this right now?

The one who's wept, questioned, grown, and glowed?

This version was written into the script before your birth.

This was the chapter that would break open your power.

The part where the plot thickens and the prophecy unfolds.

You are not a side character in someone else's narrative.

You are the headline.

The main event.

The soul who said yes to being here now.

And even when you forgot—

even when you felt lost or small or silenced—

the real you was still writing.

Because no matter how wild the plot twists got,

your higher self kept scripting redemption.

You're the scribe of your sacred story.

The vessel of your own volume.

The scroll is YOU—unfolding in pages of pain, triumph, learning, laughter, and becoming.

And the moment you realized you could write it differently?

That was the moment everything changed.

So write.

Rewrite.

Speak.

Sing.

Create.

Reclaim your authorship.

This chapter of YOU was always meant to be written.

And now it is.

Universal Law:

Law of Creation — You are a conscious co-creator. Your thoughts, words, and energy actively shape your life. You were never powerless—you were programmed to create worlds.

Scientific Insight:

Epigenetics reveals how consciousness can influence gene expression. Your beliefs, emotions, and choices are literally writing new codes into your biology.

Journal Reflection:

What chapter are you ready to write now that you've reclaimed your pen? What story will your next version tell?

Affirmation:

I am the author of my divine story. Each page I write aligns with the truth of who I am.

Heaven on Earth

Poem

I must interrupt your scheduled programming

Intercept invisible waves, your cortex base, signal jamming

Yoga Breathe. Regulate your algorithm

Inject your prana with ancient mysticism

Detox your being with the unseen Spiritual cleanse

Remove the toxins, from within

This may seem strange at first

cuz we've been brainwashed from birth

Conditioned to the point, our lives we live cursed

We had no clue, we're trained that way

Stay on bended knee and pray

And never seek what we need from inward

Forced to believe we are minute common folk and N-words

Nothing more and always less

Fill our minds up with defeat and stress

So these will be the things we manifest

Under duress, with sheeple and all the rest

Packs herded to be disconnected

Caught in the illusion of the separate

That's the secret weapon of deception

Caught in paradigms and limited perception

Severed and decapitated, mentally naked,

Intoxicated with misinformation, totally wasted

Running around like a chicken with its head cut off

Crippled us like when they took Chicken George's foot off

Now it's time to dust off books of ancient teachings

To reach the masses and thaw the freezing

Stuck in one place, cryogenics mentality

To realize what's real of this reality

It's not just what you can see and feel is quantitative

When this holographic universe was created

To God status, we're elevated

On planes of collective consciousness, demonstrated

But as frequencies lowered and vibrations got slower

Real knowledge is kept by the rich, so our spirit gets poorer

Enlighten those in the dark, Illuminate their shine

And spark a pure light on the wick of your mind

And find your way out of the rabbit hole

Coasting down this slippery slope with your soul

The gold that you hold controls the rules, as you see fit

Keep a compass with your judgment is how I interpret it

The human condition, we need to act with urgentness

We need to fix it cuz its 13 ways to worsen it

The way we gettin' played, we cursing it

We're oblivious to what, when and how the serpent bit

Drunk off the residual poison of our great, great, great grandmothers oppressors

From killers, rapist, to manipulative molesters

And deprived of the antidote, only to be pacified with anecdotes

Literally Humans being enslaved by animals

To confuse our reality with fantasy

Time to decode the message for every man to see

In plain sight,

Activate your response, aviate or fight

Map your destination in this electromagnetic universe

We draw everything into our existence like penning a verse

With persistence and no resistance, good or bad, whether we see it

This predates Sanskrit, the Mayans and Egypt

Before Atlanteans or Sumerians

Now were divine slaves led by Luciferians

Mesmerized with mindless entertainment and desperate despair

Create problems out of thin air, disconnected from care

Now the only gesture or effort put in is a "Like or Share"

Genuine connection is obsolete like tech every 2 months

ADD attention spans, as everyone puts on a front

Narcissism and ego rules, No morals is "so cool"

Highlight reel of Rental Car and Rented Jewels

Free willed puppet fools have no idea the truth is proven

And unmoved in the right direction, but you can

It's easier not to think, and just "take their word for it"

This is as good as it gets, rewind to fast forward

Same song that's been playing for years, same chorus

But the secret is we're divine creatures with unlimited God sources

So your conscience, has to be conscious of it's TORUS

Not the Bull, the full lung of God's breath,

No sorceress

Expand and contract, in my center then outward, it courses

Recycle itself in energetic skin, that's porous seen by Horus

These forces are at work regardless, that's why I work on it the hardest

To have it work for me like an employee, whose paycheck is marvelous

More than the extra mile, it travels the Farthest

To harness the Light of the darkness

Balance my center, then enter myself, in the oneness of OM

Because within my spirit is home

I get group hugs from Me, Myself and I belong

As long as I come in, I will never be alone

This zone is too powerful to keep solo

The gifts have to go to those around the globe who don't know

Elevate yourself until you have the glow

Then we overthrow the establishment and build it up from the dirt

So we can finally experience Heaven on Earth 1-29-16

To be human means Divine Bearer of Gifts

The Powers that Be have done an excellent job

of concealing this fact

to keep the information

to Themselves.

This poem has the purpose

to shed light on the truth that to be human is a

Beautiful and Powerful gift and we need to live out

our full potential.

Volume I – Chapter 3: The Mechanics of Manifestation

Volume I – Chapter 3: The Mechanics of Manifestation

Section 1: The Gospel of the Inner G: Your Divine Generator

Subtitle: You Are The One You Are Looking For

> "You don't need to search for energy—you are the energy. You are the Inner G."
> —Idara Umana

What is the Inner G?

Inner G is not just a clever wordplay on "energy"—it's the reveal of the real power source you've had inside you all along. It is:

- Inner God – the piece of the Creator living within you

- Inner Guidance – your intuitive GPS system

- Inner Genius – your divine intelligence and creativity

- Inner Glow – your electromagnetic frequency signature

- Inner Grounding – the sacred stabilizer within your nervous system

- Inner Generator – the energetic powerhouse that fuels your reality

When activated, your Inner G becomes your direct line to Source. It turns on your divine memory, connects you to purpose, and aligns you with the quantum field. When ignored or buried, you walk around like a phone on 2%—technically on, but barely functioning.

Scientific Insight: You Are a Living Generator

The human body generates electricity. Your brain runs on electrical impulses that fire neurons. Your heart emits the most powerful electromagnetic field in the body—detectable up to 6 feet away. According to the HeartMath Institute, the emotional vibrations you send out literally affect the energy fields of people around you.

That means your Inner G is not abstract—it's measurable.

And your thoughts, emotions, and breath are the on/off switches for your internal power grid.

Neurologically, your brain does not distinguish between imagination, memory, or real-time experience. So what you think and feel, you become. The more vividly you imagine your greatness, the more real it becomes—on a cellular level.

Universal Law: The Law of Vibration

Everything in the universe moves, vibrates, and circulates. Nothing rests. This is the Law of Vibration, one of the immutable Hermetic Laws. It states that everything—sound, light, thought, matter—has a frequency.

Your Inner G is your vibrational dial.

You attract what matches your frequency, not what matches your wish list. So when you raise your Inner G, you become a magnet for miracles.

How to Activate Your Inner G

To awaken your Inner G is to come online—like plugging into the sacred socket of Self.

Step 1: Breathe with Intention

Breath is the switch. Yoga breathing calms the SubC and lights up your nervous system. Try the 12-second breath: Inhale for 4, hold for 4, release for 4.

Step 2: Speak Life

Affirmations, declarations, prayer, song. Words are spells. When you speak from your Inner G, you code your field with truth.

Step 3: Visualize with Emotion

Use your mind's eye to see your future self. Feel it fully. Live there. Your brain will start aligning your reality to match the vision.

Step 4: Play, Laugh, Dance

Joy is fuel. The more you play, the more power you generate. Remember: fun is a frequency.

Step 5: Stay Ready So You Don't Have to Get Ready

Rehearse how you'll handle trials before they arrive. When you stay grounded in Inner G, chaos can't take the wheel.

Inner G vs Outer World

The world teaches you to outsource your power:

- To status

- To money

- To institutions

- To religion

But Inner G flips the script. You become the source. You stop asking permission to be powerful. You stop reacting to life and start commanding it.

What Happens When You Live from Inner G?

You begin to:

- Manifest faster, with ease

- Discern truth from illusion

- Protect your peace like royalty

- Magnetize divine connections

- Glow, even in the dark

You become a vibrational architect, building reality from the inside out. No longer a reactor. Now a Creator.

Affirmation:

"I am powered by my Inner G—divine, unstoppable, and connected to the All."

Inner G Reflection:

Where have I been outsourcing my power, and how can I call it back today?

Volume I – Chapter 3: The Mechanics of Manifestation

Section 2: The Man-chine: Divine Technology in Human Form

Subtitle: You Are The Blueprint

> "You are not a machine. You are a Man-chine—God-coded, Spirit-breathed, biologically electric, and cosmically connected."
> —Idara Umana

What is the Man-chine?

The Man-chine is your spiritual hardware—your biological body infused with divine coding. It's where man (consciousness) meets machine (vessel). You are not just flesh and bones. You are spiritual circuitry in motion.

You are the original intelligent device.

You breathe air like a fan system.

You run on current like a battery.

You store memories like a hard drive.

You download visions like Wi-Fi.

You have a processor (brain), a transmitter (heart), and a power source (spirit).

This body isn't a burden—it's a technology.

You are not broken—you're just out of sync.

And the moment you learn to operate this machine correctly…? Baby, it's God Mode unlocked.

Scientific Insight: Your Body is Electric

The nervous system is an electrical communication network made of neurons that fire electrochemical signals. Your cells are voltage-based. Your heart generates an electromagnetic field stronger than any other organ. Even your DNA coils and reacts to frequency and intention.

According to Dr. Joe Dispenza, thought + emotion = an energetic signal broadcast into the quantum field.

Your internal state determines external experience— because your Man-chine is broadcasting 24/7.

Even your gut (often called your "second brain") sends signals to the brain—impacting mood, clarity, immunity, and intuitive knowing.

Universal Law: The Law of Correspondence

"As above, so below. As within, so without."

This law confirms that the microcosm reflects the macrocosm. Your body is a mirror of the cosmos. The human form is not just symbolic—it's a literal map of divine mechanics.

Your chakras = energy portals.

Your spine = the staff of divine current.

Your breath = the fuel line.

Your voice = the sound programmer.

Your skin = your sensor array.

To master your Man-chine is to master reality.

The Man-chine Operating System

System	Spiritual Function	Earthly Action
Mind	Processor	Thought Input
Heart	Transmitter	Emotion Output
Breath	Activation Key	Frequency Control
Voice	Command Console	Spoken Manifestation
Gut	Guidance System	Inner Knowing
Skin	Sensor	Vibrational Feedback

Most people are using outdated code, reacting on emotional autopilot, or carrying virus scripts (trauma, societal programming, negative beliefs).

To reprogram your Man-chine, you must:

- Delete corrupted files (limiting beliefs, past trauma)

- Update software (new thoughts, affirmations, breathing practices)

- Activate apps (power poses, mudras, meditation, visualization)

- Install firewalls (boundaries, conscious inputs, soul hygiene)

The Battery Concept: Energy as Currency

Your Man-chine runs on prana, oxygen, emotion, and focus.

Just like a phone loses charge, so do you.

Just like a phone gets viruses, so do you.

And just like a phone needs updates, YOU do too.

That's why grounding, breathwork, sleep, water, and solitude are spiritual maintenance practices—not luxuries.

What Happens When You Master Your Man-chine?

You become:

- A conscious creator, not a passive reactor

- A living blueprint of health, harmony, and high-frequency

- A sovereign being, no longer a slave to "earthly matters"

- A walking God-signal, vibrating truth into form

Man-chine Mastery Practices

- Breathwork: Override the system with deep, rhythmic breathing

- Sound Healing: Tune your frequency with binaural beats, singing bowls, or mantra

- Affirmation Loops: Recode your thoughts through repetition

- Visualization Routines: Pre-program desired outcomes in the quantum

- Sacred Movement: Use dance, yoga, or power poses to channel energy

- Energetic Hygiene: Detox your field daily (media, food, conversations, tech)

Journal Prompt:

Where have I allowed my Man-chine to run on outdated or external programming—and how can I reclaim the controls?

Affirmation:

"I am a Divine Man-chine. I operate in harmony with Spirit, and I master my reality from within."

Volume I – Chapter 3: The Mechanics of Manifestation

Section 3: Vibration First, Then Matter

Subtitle: The Unseen Tools To Build Mansions

"The air is alive, and it forms thoughts into matter like clay. We are divine potters."

You are not just a body walking through space—you are a vibrating signal wrapped in flesh. A broadcast tower of divine frequency. Every thought you think, every emotion you feel, is a transmission sent out into the quantum field. And the quantum field? It responds like a faithful servant, reflecting your internal vibration back to you in the form of reality. Thought becomes thing. Emotion becomes environment. It's not magic. It's not mystery. It's math.

The quantum field is alive. It's the intelligent, invisible matrix that connects all living things. Some call it the unified field. Others call it the mind of God. You interact with it constantly, whether you know it or not. Every wish, every worry, every word is a ripple in that field—and ripples become waves, and waves become walls, and walls become the reality you live inside of.

Your thoughts? They're magnetic.

Your emotions? They're electric.

Together, they create your electromagnetic signature—
a frequency that carries instructions for what the
universe should deliver.

When you think a thought, especially with strong
emotion, it sends out a coded request. If the thought is
repeated often enough, and charged with enough
feeling, the field starts arranging things on your behalf.
You don't have to "force" anything into existence—
you align with it, and it arrives.

But here's the catch:

The field doesn't respond to what you say you want.

It responds to the energy you sit in.

You can say "I'm abundant," but if you feel broke,
stressed, and unworthy, your dominant signal is lack—
and the field echoes it back. That's why awareness of
your vibration is everything.

Thoughts + Emotions = Frequency

Frequency = Signal

Signal = Manifestation Blueprint

And because the quantum field is non-linear, you
don't have to wait for time to pass to "earn" what you
desire. You tune into it now, in advance. That's how
you collapse time. You become the person who
already has it—energetically—and reality starts to
reflect that version of you.

This is why breathwork, meditation, ritual, and inner
dialogue matter so much. They're not fluff. They're

tools of quantum technology—ways to shift your frequency, alter your signal, and write new code into the simulation.

You are a living transmitter.

The field is listening.

What song are you broadcasting?

Before it forms, it vibrates.

That's the first law of manifestation. Nothing appears in your life without first vibrating into place. Vibration is the unseen sculptor behind all visible form.

Everything begins as frequency. Thought is vibration. Emotion is vibration. Words are vibration. And vibration becomes matter when it is held long enough, strong enough, and intentionally enough.

I used to think manifestation was just about saying affirmations or visualizing—until I realized that what I truly feel, I truly form. The law is not based on lip service—it's based on energetic broadcast.

The Quantum Field doesn't read your grammar, it reads your frequency.

This is why trauma cycles repeat—not because we're broken, but because our vibration is recycling the same energetic blueprint. The shift happens when you choose to vibrate higher, not just think happier.

Universal Law: Law of Vibration

Everything in the universe moves, vibrates, and travels in circular patterns. This includes our thoughts, emotions, and intentions. High vibration attracts high results.

Scientific Insight:
Our heart emits an electromagnetic field measurable several feet beyond the body. Our emotions generate electricity. Our thoughts generate magnetism. Together, they create the field that shapes our experiences.

Journal Prompt:

What thought or emotion am I rehearsing daily that may be shaping my reality without my permission? What has your dominant vibration been lately—and what kind of life has it been creating around you?

I am a divine frequency tower, broadcasting my highest truth into the quantum field. My thoughts are focused, my emotions are aligned, and my life reflects my inner command.

Affirmation:

I align my vibration with truth, love, clarity, and bold expectancy. I am the architect of energy that becomes form.

Poetic Spiritual Formulas for Manifestation

The Spoken Word as Quantum Command

> "Speak it like a song, think it like a code, feel it like it's already yours—and it must obey."

These aren't just affirmations. These are encoded verbal technologies—designed to recalibrate your energy, command your field, and align your vibration with the quantum realm.

Each line is a spiritual formula, a spoken equation that merges breath, belief, sound, rhythm, intention, and Universal Law. This is where science and poetry kiss.

EXAMPLES (Original Formulas from My Epiphanies):

- "What I see in my mind, I will hold in my hands."

  (Law of Mentalism + Law of Attraction)

- "My breath is my yes. My exhale is my Ase'."

(Law of Vibration + Law of Correspondence)

- "Energy is spiritual currency—spend it like your soul depends on it."

  (Law of Compensation)

- "I magnetize what I fantasize, and I fantasize wisely."

  (Law of Attraction + Law of Cause & Effect)

- "Be it until you see it."

  (Law of Assumption)

- "God is the Wi-Fi. My belief is the password."

  (Law of Perpetual Transmutation)

- "My words wear clothes—so I dress them in destiny."

  (Law of Gender: Word as seed, feeling as womb)

- "My Inner G creates my outer geometry."

(Law of Vibration + Law of Divine Oneness)

Scientific Insight:

Neuroscience shows that repeating rhythmic phrases with emotional charge creates neural resonance—a feedback loop in the brain that reinforces belief and behavior. When spoken with breath and belief, these formulas become mantra codes that program the subconscious mind and rewrite your internal operating system.

Universal Laws:

These poetic formulas are built on:

- Law of Vibration – spoken words create frequency

- Law of Mentalism – thought is the beginning of all form

- Law of Action – speaking is a divine action

- Law of Correspondence – as you think and speak, so shall it be

Journal Prompt:

Write your own poetic formula. What do you need to encode today?

Example starter:

"Through breath and belief, I call in _____."

Affirmation:

"My words are spells, my voice is sacred, and my frequency is holy. I manifest with rhythm, power, and truth."

Volume I – Chapter 3: The Mechanics of Manifestation

Section 4: The Mental Garden, Frequency Thieves & the Energy Vortex

Subtitle: How to Guard Your Mind, Protect Your Vibe, and Restore Divine Flow

---

1. The Mental Garden

> "You are the gardener. Your thoughts are the seeds. Your life is the harvest."

Your mind is not a landfill. It's a garden.

And what grows there depends on what you plant—and what you allow to root.

Every belief, every memory, every phrase you say on repeat is a seed.

Some were planted with love. Others were dropped into your soil without your consent—by trauma, by society, by generational patterns.

The weeds? Those are self-doubt, fear, comparison, emotional residue, and outdated paradigms that sprouted from unattended thoughts.

But here's the sacred truth: you are the gardener and the gatekeeper.

If you don't guard your mental gates, any stray energy can sneak in and claim territory.

> **Scientific Insight**: Neuroplasticity proves that repeated thoughts rewire your brain and alter behavior. Thoughts are living programs—they either fortify your system or drain it.

> **Universal Law**: The Law of Mentalism – All is mind; you must cultivate your internal world before your outer world can flourish.

2. Frequency Thieves

> "Your energy is spiritual currency—protect it like your soul depends on it."

Just like your wallet can get pickpocketed, your frequency can get hijacked.

Your energy field (aura) is like Wi-Fi—it broadcasts and receives signals.

But when you're around low vibrational people, chaotic environments, or tech overload, your signal gets scrambled.

> That's when Frequency Thieves come in:

- Toxic conversations

- Draining relationships

- Media that embeds fear

- EMF radiation from phones, Wi-Fi, and devices

These "energy vampires" don't just take your time—they take your vibration.

They leave you tired, off balance, second guessing yourself, and mentally foggy.

> I witnessed this firsthand at a live lecture with Dr. Delbert Blair.
> He showed how using a cell phone immediately reduced physical strength.
> Then he restored energy by spinning his hand in a clockwise vortex—literally creating an energy field that recharged his body.

He proved that devices drain us, but frequency and movement can heal.

Scientific Insight:

- Bioelectricity: the human body runs on electrical charge.

- EMF interference scrambles your natural frequency.

- Vortex motion—circular hand movements—amplify energy flow by mimicking natural sacred geometry (like the torus field).

3. The Energy Vortex

> "When your field is clear, you become the charger—not the one who always needs charging."

The energy vortex is your built-in restoration system.

By creating conscious movement patterns—such as spinning your hand clockwise, breathwork, or intentional body alignment—you activate your personal energy field, similar to a torus or spiral galaxy.

This field pulls in fresh energy and releases blockages. It is:

- Your protection shield

- Your amplifier

- Your signal booster to the Divine Wi-Fi

Ritual Insight:
Try the 12-second vortex breath:

1. Inhale 4 seconds (draw energy in)

2. Hold 4 seconds (swirl it in your body)

3. Exhale 4 seconds (release what doesn't serve)

4. Spin your dominant hand clockwise 3 times while visualizing golden light

This reboots your man-chine and fortifies your aura. You become less reactive, more magnetic, and clear enough to hear divine guidance.

Universal Law: The Law of Vibration + The Law of Rhythm – Everything moves in cycles. Use the spiral to return to center and create momentum from stillness.

ORIGINAL EPIPHANIES :

- "People are walking around with their hand of cards showing and everybody can see it."

- "The mind is a garden and society keeps throwing weeds into our soil."

- "I learned how to reset my energy field using a vortex—I saw it with my own eyes. Dr. Delbert Blair showed me."

- "You are like a battery. And if you don't recharge on purpose, the world will drain you and call you crazy for being dead."

Journal Prompt:

What thoughts or people have I allowed to take root in my garden? What frequency thieves do I need to block? How can I spin my vortex and recharge today?"

Affirmation:

"I guard my mental garden. I block frequency thieves. I reset my field with sacred breath and vortex power. I am charged by divine energy. My frequency is my fortress.

Energy Vortex Hand Motion

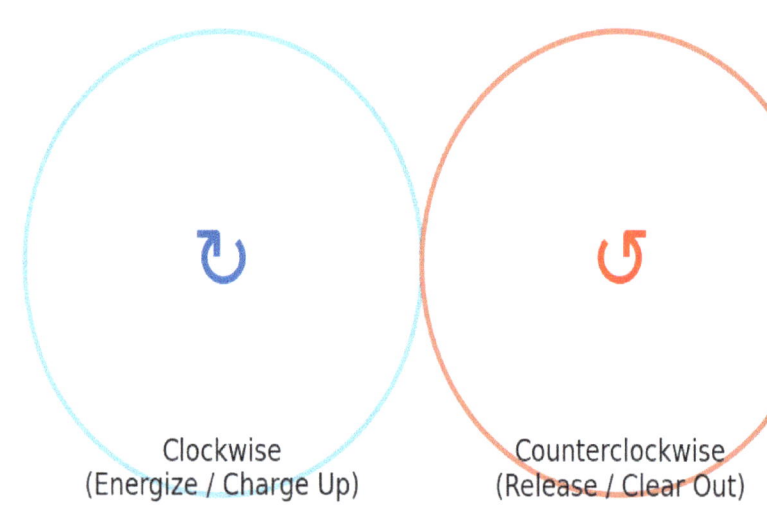

Clockwise
(Energize / Charge Up)

Counterclockwise
(Release / Clear Out)

How Tech Affects the Energy Body & Restoration Flow

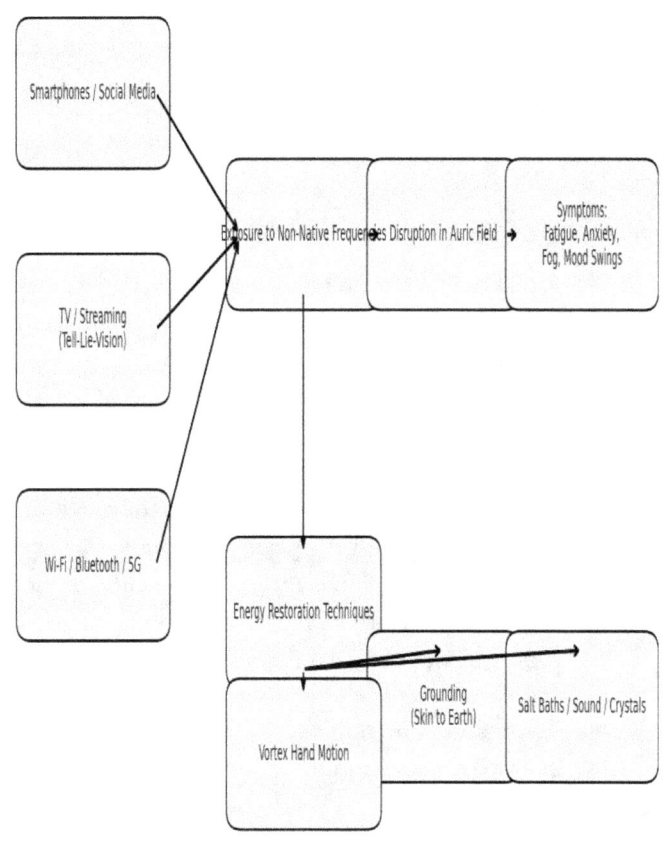

Volume I – Chapter 3: The Mechanics of Manifestation

Section 5: Rituals & Affirmations

Subtitle: Sacred Repetition, Spiritual Precision

"Words are spells. Movements are codes. When ritual meets intention, reality obeys."

Ritual isn't just routine—it's rhythm. It's your soul performing ceremony with the divine, even in the mundane.

When you ritualize something, you're creating an energetic groove. And that groove becomes a highway. A fast lane between intention and manifestation. Every affirmation you speak with conviction, every candle you light with clarity, every gesture, mudra, or sacred movement you repeat—it's all part of how you program your personal field.

Affirmations are not just cute sayings on a vision board. They are vibrational codes that realign your neurons, rewire your brain, and retune your frequency. But they must be felt, not just said. A hollow affirmation is like yelling into the wind. But a charged affirmation—spoken from the gut, believed by the heart, and repeated by the mind—is a spell cast with divine accuracy.

Rituals can be simple or elaborate. It's the intention that gives them power. Brushing your hair with love, lighting incense while you journal, pouring water and whispering gratitude—these are not empty acts. They're sacred acts. Acts that tell the universe: "I'm listening. I'm co-creating. I am ready."

Here are a few forms you can use:

- Mirror Work: Stand in front of your reflection and speak to yourself with love, authority, and clarity. Say the affirmations you need to hear.

- Candle Charging: Light a candle with a specific color frequency (green for abundance, blue for clarity, red for courage) while speaking your intention aloud.

- Water Spells: Speak your desires into a glass or bottle of water and drink it mindfully. Let the coded water become one with your cells.

- Anointing: Rub oil (like frankincense or lavender) on your pulse points and speak your affirmations as you touch each place. This becomes a spiritual activation.

- Breathwork Ritual: Breathe in your power. Hold it. Speak your truth on the exhale. Repeat until the body feels it too.

Journal Question:

What daily or weekly rituals help me align with my highest self—and how can I turn more of my everyday moments into sacred ones?

Affirmation:

"Every word I speak with intention becomes law. Every act I perform with love becomes ritual. I am the altar, the priest, and the prophecy fulfilled."

Volume I – Chapter 3: The Mechanics of Manifestation

Section 6: Power 5 Affirmations

Subtitle: The Sacred Reset for Mind, Breath, and Manifestation

> "Sometimes all you need is 5 words to flip the frequency, shift the spirit, and rewire the vibe."

CONCEPT OVERVIEW:

The Power 5 are short, potent affirmations—five words or less—that act like spiritual override codes.

They're not just affirmations. They are:

- Emergency resets for the nervous system

- Spoken passwords for divine access

- Emotional interrupters for spiraling thoughts

- Vibrational focus points during manifestation work or yoga breath

- Command phrases that train the subconscious

These affirmations are designed to be said during:

- 12-second breathwork (Inhale, hold, exhale)

- Triggered moments (anger, fear, doubt)

- Daily mantra practice

- Visualization rituals

WHY "5"?

The number 5 in sacred geometry represents:

- Balance between the physical (4) and the spiritual (1)

- Humanity (five fingers, five senses, five extremities)

- Change, movement, grace, and divine will

Speaking five-word affirmations locks the energy in place—like a spiritual seal or vibration code. You are commanding the frequency to stabilize, rise, or redirect. Have 5 statements ready to repeat and fire away to rewire your mind for these moments.

SCIENTIFIC INSIGHT:

Psychologically, shorter affirmations bypass mental resistance. The brain is more likely to believe and retain short, rhythmic, emotionally charged phrases.

Spoken affirmations create measurable electromagnetic signals, altering the body's energetic field (especially when paired with breath and visualization). That's why Power 5 works on a chemical and quantum level.

UNIVERSAL LAWS IN MOTION:

- Law of Action – Your word is a divine act

- Law of Vibration – Spoken words set energetic tone

- Law of Cause and Effect – Your internal shift creates external ripple

- Law of Assumption – You declare it, you become it

EXAMPLES OF POWER 5:

- I am God in action.

- I release and rise higher.

- Peace lives in me now.

- This breath is my prayer.

- I magnetize what I believe.

- Joy is my frequency today.

- Love, Grace, Light, and Power.

- No weapon formed shall prosper.

- I already have the answer.

- It is already done. Ase' and Amen.

HOW TO USE:

1. Breathe deeply for 12 seconds

2. On the exhale, speak your Power 5

3. Repeat as needed until the emotion shifts or clarity returns

This is your spiritual steering wheel when life tries to knock you off center.

Journal Prompt:

What Power 5 phrase do I need to carry today? What energy do I want to program into my breath and mind?"

Affirmation:

"My words are power. My breath is divine. My thoughts are spells. I choose what I embody."

Volume I – Chapter 3: The Mechanics of Manifestation

Section 7: Breathwork & Sound Healing

Subtitle: Venting With Air Not Anger and Vibing With Creation

"Your breath is not just air—it's a power tool."

It's the bridge between spirit and body, the code that calms the nervous system, and the gateway to divine alignment. When I discovered breathwork, I realized I had been shallow-breathing my way through life— barely tapping into my power source.

Sound takes this even deeper. I once laid down with singing bowls over my chakras and felt something unlock in my DNA. My cells were dancing, reorganizing. It wasn't imagination—it was vibration tuning my system.

Our ancestors knew this. They used chants, drums, humming, bells, and frequencies to realign with Source.

Universal Law: Law of Resonance
When two objects vibrate at different frequencies, the one with the stronger vibration can shift the other to match its frequency. Breath and sound can retune your entire field.

Scientific Insight:

Cymatics shows us that sound creates structure—geometric patterns in sand, water, and cells. Breathwork increases oxygen flow, balances pH, and activates the vagus nerve, bringing the body into coherence.

Journal Prompt:

When was the last time I consciously used breath or sound to shift my state? How did I feel before and after?

Affirmation:

With every breath, I tune my body to harmony. My voice and vibration are healing technologies, and I use them with intention.

Volume I – Chapter 3: The Mechanics of Manifestation

Section 8: The Golden Time of Night

Subtitle: Unlocking The Treasure Chest of The Cosmos

"There's a sacred pocket of time when the world is quiet—but the Universe is loud."

Between 2 AM and 5 AM lies the golden time of night, the spiritual sweet spot where the veil is thin, the subconscious is open, and divine downloads flow with ease. I didn't learn this from a textbook. I lived it. Some of my deepest insights, healing, and creative ideas came during those hours—sometimes waking me from sleep like spirit tapping on my shoulder.

This time window isn't just poetic—it's biological and metaphysical. Your brain transitions into delta and theta waves, the deep states where reprogramming and spiritual connection happen. It's the realm where spirit whispers and the ego sleeps.

So instead of fighting insomnia, I learned to lean in. To breathe. To write. To listen. It became a portal of peace, not panic.

Universal Law: Law of Rhythm
All things move in cycles and seasons—including our mind states. Night is not an absence of power; it is a

shift in frequency.

Scientific Insight:
During sleep, the glymphatic system clears toxins from the brain. Theta waves enhance intuition, creativity, and neuroplasticity. The pineal gland (linked to the third eye) is most active during these early hours, influenced by melatonin and cosmic rhythm.

Journal Prompt:

What thoughts, dreams, or insights visit me during the early hours? What might my soul be trying to say when the world is asleep?

Affirmation:

I honor the quiet power of the night. In stillness, I receive divine instruction. In darkness, I remember my light.

Volume I – Chapter 3: The Mechanics of Manifestation
Section 9: Manifesting the Frequency of the Lottery

Subtitle: It's Not the Numbers—It's the Vibration

"Sometimes you don't win the lottery—you become it."

One day, I was having a conversation with God—real talk, spirit-to-soul. And I asked about all the people trying to manifest winning the lottery. Not just for greed, but survival. Desire. Hope. I wanted to understand the energy behind it.

And what I heard back was clear:

"I gave everyone a winning lottery ticket, you were born with it. A God given talent, all you have to do is cash it in."

Whew.

See, people focus on manifesting the thing—the ticket, the numbers, the prize. But in truth, manifestation aligns through vibration, not physical outcome. When you're asking to "win the lottery," what you're really asking for is freedom, ease, overflow, a life of dreams unlocked. You're asking to feel secure, celebrated, and fully resourced.

And sometimes, God doesn't send the exact event.

God sends the energetic equivalent.

That was the download. And I felt it deeply because—truthfully? I already feel like I hit the lottery. Not because of a check. Not because of a jackpot. But because of my gifts.

My insight. My voice. My creativity. My resilience.

These gifts are wealth.

And the moment I realized that I could translate my divine inheritance into income, I understood what the download meant.

I didn't need the ticket.

I became the vibration.

Scientific Insight: Frequency Matching and the Quantum Field

Quantum physics confirms that energy attracts energy of like frequency. When you emit the feeling of wealth, your field aligns with experiences that match that vibration—whether it shows up as a windfall, an opportunity, a new connection, or a creative gift finally paying off.

This is how the law of resonance works.

It's not always literal—it's energetic alignment. You don't manifest what you want. You manifest what you are vibrating with.

Universal Law: The Law of Attraction + The Law of Correspondence

The Law of Attraction teaches that like attracts like. The Law of Correspondence reminds us that outer experiences mirror inner states. When you embody the frequency of "having won," the Universe reflects that back in the form that best supports your soul path—not always a check, but always a match.

Personal Experience

I used to imagine what I would do if I won the lottery. Like many people, I thought that was the only way out. But once I started leaning into my spiritual gifts, I had another realization:

What if my gifts were the jackpot?

What if all the pain, all the insight, all the power I've gained was the true million-dollar blessing?

And what if the money was just waiting for me to realize that first?

That shifted everything.

I stopped begging for the prize and started becoming the prize.

Ritual: Tune Into the Frequency of Winning

Use this ritual to shift from desire to embodiment—feeling like you've already won.

What You'll Need:

- A quiet space

- A vision board or blank page

- A mirror or your own voice

Steps:

1. Sit still and recall how you would feel if you had just won the lottery. Feel it. Embody it.

2. Write down what you imagine that version of you would do, wear, feel, and say.

3. Now go to the mirror and say:

   "I already carry the vibration of overflow. My gifts are my wealth. I am the frequency of winning."

4. End with a smile or laugh—embodying joy is the energetic receipt.

Journal Prompt:

What would your life look like if you fully believed your gifts were the jackpot?

Affirmation:

"I am not chasing the lottery—I am the lottery. My gifts are divine currency, and my wealth flows through purpose, passion, and power."

Volume I – Chapter 3: The Mechanics of Manifestation

Section 10: The Mirror on the Inside of You: Life is a Mirror

Subtitle: Don't Fake It Until You Make It, Be It Until You See It

Life doesn't happen to you—it reflects you

Once I realized that people, situations, and even delays were mirrors, not punishments, everything changed. I stopped asking "Why me?" and started asking, "What is this showing me?"

The universe doesn't play favorites—it plays frequencies. Your outer world reflects your inner world. If there's chaos outside, there's probably some chaos inside. If blessings are blocked, there may be a belief that doesn't feel worthy of receiving.

It's not about blame—it's about awareness. You're not cursed. You're coded.

Universal Law: Law of Correspondence
As within, so without. As above, so below. Your external reality is a mirror of your internal state.

Scientific Insight:
Cognitive behavioral studies show that perception shapes experience. Neural pathways created by

repeated beliefs cause the brain to filter reality in ways that match those beliefs—reinforcing your internal world as your outer truth.

Journal Prompt:

What recurring patterns in my life might be mirroring an outdated belief or emotional frequency I'm still carrying?

Affirmation:

I see the world through the lens of clarity and healing. I shift my inner truth and watch the world transform around me.

Volume I – Chapter 3: The Mechanics of Manifestation

Section 11: The Sacred Technology of Sex: Power, Pleasure & Manifestation

Subtitle: Fueling the Fantasy: The Sacred Technology of Sex"

> "Sex is power-generating technology. It's not dirty. It's divine. It's technology that turns our bodies into fantasy manifesting factories…"

Let's get this straight: sex is not just about physical pleasure. It's one of the most powerful energetic tools humans have been gifted—and like any tool, it can be misused or mastered.

We were never taught the full truth of sexual energy. We were taught to hide it, fear it, or indulge recklessly in it—but rarely to honor it.

When aligned with breath, intention, and heart-centered awareness, sexual energy becomes a literal fuel source for manifestation. The ancients knew this. The mystics encoded it in their teachings. But society turned the sacred into shame.

Sex as a Manifestation Engine

Your body is a biological generator.

During sexual arousal, your body surges with life-force energy—the same chi or prana that animates your entire being. This is when your vibration spikes. Neural networks activate. Hormones like dopamine, oxytocin, and endorphins flood the bloodstream. In this euphoric state, your thoughts and emotions are magnified and broadcast to the quantum field at lightning speed.

If you set a clear intention at the height of this energy—whether alone or with a partner—you are essentially saying to the universe:

"THIS is the frequency I want more of."

But here's the key: you must be clear. Don't set a frequency based in lust, lack, or loneliness. That's what you'll manifest more of.

Set it in wholeness, joy, love, gratitude, purpose. And feel it as if it's already yours.

How It Works (Energetically)

- Sexual arousal activates the sacral chakra, the seat of creation

- When combined with intentional breathwork, it pulls energy upward through the spine

- The pineal gland (third eye) begins to tingle, receive, and radiate new frequencies

- The heart field expands, aligning emotion with thought

- This union between heart, mind, and sacral energy becomes God energy in motion

This is the metaphysical version of alchemy. Turning primal energy into spiritual gold.

Scientific Insight:

- Sex boosts neuroplasticity and strengthens intention pathways in the brain.

- During orgasm, the prefrontal cortex quiets, allowing the subconscious to come forward—making it an ideal time to plant seeds for manifestation.

- Visualizations during climax anchor new mental associations and emotional states into long-term memory and energetic fields.

Universal Laws:

- Law of Vibration: Arousal and pleasure raise
  your frequency. What you broadcast, you
  attract.

- Law of Perpetual Transmutation: Energy
  never dies—it transforms. Sexual energy can
  transmute into creative force, healing, or
  divine manifestation.

- Law of Correspondence: As within, so
  without. The inner union of pleasure and
  purpose births external results.

HOLY SEXUALITY IS:

- Sovereign – whether alone or with a partner, your body is your sacred space

- Intentional – it's not about the act, but the alignment

- Creative – you're not just creating pleasure, you're creating reality

- Healing – stored trauma in the sacral can be released through breath + love

- Divine – the orgasm is not just climax, it's communion

PRACTICE: The Sacred Solo Ritual (Short Version)

1. Set the intention: Choose a feeling or reality you want to embody.

2. Visualize it clearly. Feel it in your body.

3. Use breath to guide your energy upward through the spine.

4. As climax nears, repeat a Power 5 like:

"It is already done."

5. At the peak, imagine your manifestation bursting into the universe, like fireworks made of fact.

6. Rest. Receive. Recharge.

Journal Prompt:

"What beliefs have I inherited about sexuality, and how can I rewrite them to align with my divinity?"

Affirmation::

"My body is sacred technology. My pleasure is permission. My intention is divine creation."

Volume I – Chapter 3: The Mechanics of Manifestation

Section 12: The Real Fountain of Youth

Subtitle: Happiness Is a Choice

"Joy is anti-aging".

Laughter, play, pleasure—these aren't just luxuries, they're longevity tools. I've seen what trauma can do to a person's face, posture, and spirit. And I've seen how healing can literally reverse it. Your glow is your testimony.

There were times I felt ten years older than I was because I carried emotional weight. When I started laughing again—like belly-aching, teary-eyed laughter—I noticed my skin looked brighter. My back stood straighter. My vibe got lighter.

This is because joy floods the body with endorphins, oxytocin, and dopamine—the real "fountain of youth" chemistry.

Universal Law: Law of Perpetual Transmutation of Energy
High vibration transforms low vibration. Joy, gratitude, and playfulness are power tools for spiritual alchemy.

Scientific Insight:
Laughter boosts immunity, decreases stress hormones, increases blood flow, and triggers the release of "feel-good" neurotransmitters. It can improve skin tone, reduce inflammation, and support heart health.

Journal Prompt: When was the last time I felt youthful, vibrant, and alive in my body—and what activity sparked that feeling?

Affirmation: I am renewed by joy. I choose laughter, lightness, and love as medicine for my body, mind, and spirit.

Volume I – Chapter 3: The Mechanics of Manifestation

Section 13: Return on Your Investment

Subtitle: Multiplying Your Spiritual Wealth (Energy is Currency)

Energy is spiritual money—spend it like your soul depends on it.

Every day, you are investing. Not just with money—but with thought, time, attention, and emotion. And just like any smart investor, you need to check what kind of returns you're getting from where you're spending your energy. And the universe? It always pays back—with interest. The question is: what are you investing in? Fear? Doubt? Complaining? Or clarity, alignment, and bold vision?

See, energy is currency. And your reality is the receipt.

Every thought you think, every vibe you entertain, every second you spend—it's all spiritual capital. And you don't get to skip the return. The universe is a divine accountant. It always balances the books. You will always receive a return on your investment—good, bad, or neutral. That's law.

So let me break this down:

You can't wake up every day pouring your thoughts into fear, guilt, comparison, or hopelessness and then be shocked when a storm shows up at your door instead of rainbows. You invested in the storm. You deposited anxiety into your mental bank account every morning. You spent hours replaying "what ifs" and worst-case scenarios like a mental movie marathon. And the field delivered what you ordered.

And the field will always deliver. It's not personal. It's mathematical.

🐾 "It's not a mystery. It's math."

Think about it. You wouldn't take your hard-earned paycheck and blow it on junk you don't want. So why do we spend our most valuable resource—our focus—on worry, drama, low-vibe loops, and things that drain us?

Would you pay $1000 for a broken TV? Then why pay your peace for someone else's chaos?

Here's the spiritual principle:

Your attention is sacred. Your time is holy. Your focus is power.

Spend it like it matters. Because it does.

Let's talk about mental budgeting.

When your mind starts veering into lack, fear, or spirals of unworthiness, that's your cue to recalculate.

Just like a GPS reroutes you when you've taken a wrong turn, your feelings are the alert system that tells you something's off. If it doesn't feel good—it's a signal to reset.

That's when you pull out the Power Fist —your arsenal of 5 spiritual affirmations to punch through the fog and reclaim your frequency.

Examples:

- I am powerful beyond measure.

- I am a magnet for miracles.

- I am chosen, divine, and protected.

- I am more than enough, and I always have been.

- I am the author of my reality—and I'm flipping the script today.

Use them like spiritual brass knuckles. Speak them until the static clears. This is how you interrupt the loop and make a different deposit into the quantum field.

Let's go deeper with a few analogies:

Energy as Spiritual Money

If money is a medium of exchange in the material world, then energy is the same in the spiritual world. Your thoughts and feelings are constantly paying for experiences. So if you're spending your energy on "I'm not good enough," don't be surprised when experiences show up that confirm that belief. That's what you paid for.

Emotional ROI

If an emotion is costing you your peace, your joy, or your hope—what's the return? Is the emotional rant worth the vibrational dip? Every emotional state is a purchase. Be intentional about your spending.

The Garden of Your Mind

Whatever you plant—grows. If you water fear, fear grows. If you nurture faith, faith grows. Understand the statement "Energy goes where attention flows". If you want a garden full of beauty, be mindful of what you're planting each day.

So, let's flip it.

Invest in peace.

Invest in play.

Invest in what you love.

Invest in your healing.

Invest in bold-ass dreams that scare your small self and light your big self on fire.

Because you are not just a consumer of life—you are a creator of it.

And if you can create your own suffering by accident...

You sure as hell can create your joy on purpose.

Universal Law: Law of Cause and Effect
Every action has a reaction. What you invest energetically returns as form and experience. You don't escape the harvest—you meet it.

Scientific Insight:
Neural plasticity means your thoughts rewire your brain. Where focus goes, energy flows—literally. Chronic negative thinking leads to chronic stress. Positive mental focus leads to healing, vision, and vitality.

Journal Prompt:

What have I been "paying into" that hasn't given me a divine return—and what would I rather invest in moving forward?

Affirmation:

"I spend my energy like sacred currency. I invest in peace, power, and possibility—and I receive it multiplied. I am my highest return."

Volume I – Chapter 3: The Mechanics of Manifestation

Section 14: Emotion as Frequency and Fuel

Subtitle: The Vibe That Drives the Vision

"Your emotion is the ignition key. You can have the vision, the vehicle, the map—but without fuel, you ain't going nowhere."

Thoughts send the signal.

Emotions carry the charge.

If thoughts are magnetic, pulling reality into form— then emotions are the electric current that lights the whole damn circuit.

This is where e-motion becomes what it truly is: Energy in Motion.

You can't manifest clearly if you're emotionally cluttered. You can't call in abundance while vibrating in fear. You can't declare love while simmering in resentment. That's like revving the engine while the emergency brake is still on. It doesn't move.

The emotion you hold while you visualize, affirm, or pray becomes the frequency that attracts or repels your desires.

That's why this system teaches heart and mind coherence. The feeling has to match the thought. You can say "I am abundant" all day, but if your body is trembling in anxiety or doubt, it sends static through the field.

And the quantum field doesn't speak English.

It speaks frequency.

So here's the key: Match your emotions with the reality you want—not the one you currently see.

This is where the magic lives.

Feel the joy before the love arrives.

Feel the peace before the breakthrough hits.

Feel the gratitude as if it's already done—because vibrationally, it is.

And if you struggle with this?

Use tools: breathwork, sound, music, dance, memory, even tears. Emotions are water—let them move. Let them cleanse. Let them power the signal.

You are a vibrational being.

Your emotion is your fuel.

Choose premium.

Journal Question: What emotions am I most familiar with—and are they fueling the reality I desire or blocking it? How can I become more intentional about the feelings I feed?

Affirmation: "I fuel my future with powerful emotions. Joy is my current. Love is my voltage. I am charged with divine energy, and my frequency never lies."

Volume I – Chapter 3: The Mechanics of Manifestation

Section 15: Visualization- The Mind's Eye

Subtitle: Mental Blueprinting for the Material World

"The clearest visions shape the clearest realities. See the end so vividly, the universe can't help but turn the page."

When people say "visualize what you want," they usually picture someone sitting cross-legged in a yoga pose, imagining a car or a beach house. But visualization is way deeper than daydreaming. It's mental blueprinting. A divine design phase where you sculpt the unseen in vivid, high-definition detail.

The Universe doesn't respond to vague wishes—it responds to specific vision. Think of your mind like an architect's drafting table. The clearer the design, the faster it gets built. The fuzzier the sketch, the more mistakes and miscommunications you'll run into along the way.

You must become obsessed with the vision.

Marinate in it. Orchestrate it. Adorn it. Decorate it.

Live in it before you live in it.

Analogy: Pinterest for the Soul

Your imagination is your spiritual Pinterest board.

Every time you visualize, you're pinning textures, emotions, scenes, people, and outcomes into your inner design. That board tells the Universe, "This is the vibe I want my reality to match." The stronger the emotional glue you use when pinning your desires, the faster they come.

Don't just see the house—smell the furniture, feel the carpet, taste the celebration cake in the kitchen.

Don't just see the healed relationship—hear the laughter, feel the safety, remember the love you haven't even lived yet.

Visualization isn't pretend. It's pre-living.

You're experiencing a memory from the future that you're pulling into the now.

The Power of Repetition

Repetition rewires the brain. The more you visit the vision, the more your subconscious believes it's real. Eventually, the brain will go:

> "Well, if we keep seeing this, it must be happening… better start aligning with it."

That's when opportunities, ideas, and support begin to show up seemingly out of nowhere. They aren't random. They're reflections of your internal commitment to the vision.

Use It Like a Tool — Not a Toy

This isn't about fantasizing and hoping. This is intentional construction.

You're not watching a movie. You're writing the script. Directing the scenes. Casting the players.

You're not hoping the Universe gets it right. You're saying:

> "This is what I ordered. This is what I expect. And I'll keep visualizing until the delivery arrives."

Visualization: The Blueprint of Creation

Visualization is more than wishful thinking. It's mental architecture. It's your consciousness pulling out the celestial drafting board and sketching your life into form. When you visualize clearly—with feeling, specificity, and frequency—you're feeding instructions to the quantum field. You're handing your inner God-self the script and saying: "This is what we're directing next."

But here's the secret sauce: you can't just skim the surface—you gotta read the last page.

Imagine picking up a novel and skipping to the final chapter. That final page—the triumphant moment, the resolution, the "you made it" scene—reveals what it all led to. That's how your visualization should feel. You must know how it ends, even before it begins.

What's the weather like when you walk into your dream home? What scent is in the air at your grand opening? How do your clothes fit? What shoes are you wearing? What song plays in the background? Who's texting you congratulations? How do you feel?

Get microscopic with it.

Because in manifestation, the more vividly you build the ending, the faster the beginning begins to rearrange to match. The Universe doesn't need constant repetition—it needs clear instruction and emotional investment. The feelings are the frequency. The details are the delivery address.

If you don't see it in your mind's eye, how can you expect it to arrive in your physical one?

And when you can see that final page, feel the joy of that win, taste the air of accomplishment—you become an energetic match. You shift from "asking" to "expecting," and that shift is everything. Because now, instead of hoping, you're simply waiting on the delivery of what's already yours.

Journal Prompt:
What does your highest life look like?
Don't just write about what you want—describe the details.
What do you see, smell, feel, taste, hear, wear, live in?

Who's there? What do you celebrate? What does peace look like in 4K?

If I were already living my dream life, what would my days look like? What emotions would I wake up feeling? How would I carry myself differently—and what page of that life am I ready to live today?

Affirmation:

"I build my future with bold vision. I see it, feel it, live it—and the Universe builds with me."

"I see it. I feel it. I believe it. My vision is my permission. My frequency is the invitation. And I am aligned with the reality I've already created."

Volume I – Chapter 3: The Mechanics of Manifestation

Section 16: The Wi-Fi Within

Subtitle : Your Mind, Body & Spirit Router

You can't stream your dreams on a scrambled signal. Tune in. Log on. Upload your vibration.

We live in a wireless world. Everything is invisible— but everything is connected. You trust that when you hit play, your favorite show will stream. You trust that your phone will connect to the internet, no cords required. But how often do you trust yourself to connect to the divine network that runs this whole reality?

Let's break this all the way down:

Your spirit is the device.

Your mind is the router.

Your body is the hardware.

And your emotions? That's the Wi-Fi signal strength.

If your emotions are low—doubt, fear, shame, frustration—your signal is weak, buffering, delayed. Manifestation moves slow. Downloads don't complete. You try to call your future in, but it keeps dropping like a bad connection. But when your

emotions are elevated—joy, gratitude, peace, desire—
you're on full bars. That's when miracles sync.

Let's take it further:

- The Quantum Field is like the cloud—all data,
  all outcomes, all possibilities live there.

- Your intentions are your search bar.

- Your beliefs are your firewall—if you've been
  programmed with blocks, you won't let in
  what you're asking for.

- Your visualization is the screen you see it on.

- Your heart is the power source.

You've got all the tools—you just have to learn how
to operate your spiritual technology.

Imagine waking up and not checking your phone—but
checking your signal. Ask:

Am I plugged in?
Is my channel clear?
Am I streaming love or lagging in lack?

Because just like a router can be reset, so can you.

When things go wrong in your life, it's not always the
universe punishing you. Sometimes, your router just
needs a reboot. You've been trying to stream

abundance on a frequency of fear. Trying to upload a new reality while still operating on an outdated system. You gotta clear your cache. Delete those old programs. Update your internal software.

And once you're online—baby, the whole field responds.

That's why prayer, meditation, breathwork, music, laughter, joy, and emotional mastery are vital. They're how you log in and level up. They're your energetic password to higher planes of possibility.

So the next time you feel disconnected, don't panic. Just reset.

The connection is always there. You just have to find the signal within.

Journal Prompt:

What outdated belief or emotional program have you been running on autopilot that might be weakening your connection? What would it look like to reset your inner router?

Affirmation:

I am always connected to Source. My thoughts are clear. My emotions are high. My signal is strong. I stream abundance with ease.

Volume I – Chapter 3: The Mechanics of Manifestation

Section 17: The SubC: The Shadow Speaker and Soul Guard

Subtitle: Who's The Boss Up There?

> "The subconscious is not your enemy. It's your bodyguard... the one that's been running the show while you were sleepwalking."

The Subconscious Mind, or SubC, is not some mysterious undercurrent—it's the security guard, memory bank, emergency responder, and emotional weather system of your entire human machine. It's your unspoken code. Your default program. And if you don't become aware of it, it will drive your life and call it fate. The SubC, is the invisible but powerful force scripting 90–95% of your daily behaviors. It stores every unhealed emotion, every overheard lyric, every ancestral trauma, and every unspoken belief. It doesn't judge. It doesn't reason. It simply accepts, records, and repeats.

When you're off guard, the SubC steps up. But unless you've trained it through conscious programming, it's often running on old trauma, societal noise, and low-vibrational loops.

The Role of the SubC

The SubC steps in when your Conscious Guard is off duty—when you're distracted, triggered, or caught off guard. It's reactive by nature, built to protect you, but not necessarily elevate you. That's your job.

Think of the SubC as a wild child—smart but untrained. It absorbs media, music, sarcasm, trauma, television, pop culture, relationships, thoughts, chemicals, memories—anything you were too distracted to consciously process—and files it all as truth. So when life hits a nerve, it reacts using outdated programming.

This is why most people say, "Where did that come from?" It was the SubC speaking—loud and unfiltered.

The Three Minds: Balance or Be Broken

- Subconscious (SubC): Emotional memory. Primitive patterning. Chemical addiction to emotions. Raw, reactive, and often unrefined.

- Conscious Mind: Logic. Language. Linear time. Willpower.

- Superconscious (Spirit/SuperC): Divine Insight. Intuition. Cosmic vision. Creator frequency.

The goal? Balance all three. Let the Conscious Mind be the translator. The SubC is not to be muzzled—but trained. The SuperC is the North Star, the Divine Driver.

Society = Collective Subconscious

Look around. The chaos in the streets? The mental illness, road rage, violence, irrational fear, and cancel culture? It's the unprocessed SubC of the masses playing out in public.

It's Seinfeld meets Hunger Games. A society acting out scripts written by media, trauma, and unhealed wounds—with no clear storyline, just automated reactions and theme music.

We are watching the wild SubC on display, and it's a show the elites don't have to write. They just sit back and laugh. That's the real "reality TV."

Rehearse Your Reactions

If you rehearse how to handle situations before they arrive, you won't get hijacked by the SubC when they do. The brain doesn't know the difference between imagination and real life—so visualize yourself reacting with grace, wisdom, and God-force now.

Practice being the future version of yourself. Speak from your higher self, not your inner saboteur.

The Breath Is the Bridge

When you hold your breath, you trap energy—and your SubC takes the wheel. That's when hell rises.

Use 12-second yoga breathing as a circuit breaker. Say your Power 5 Mantra in your head and reset. Breathe out static and breathe in sovereignty.

Reprogramming the SubC

The SubC isn't evil—it's programmable. But you have to starve the old code and feed it something new:

- Stop letting music and TV program your pain.

- Speak to your body like a child: with patience, repetition, and love.

- Give yourself dopamine through gratitude, not drama.

Start the upgrade by visualizing your future like it's happening now. Your SubC will believe it—and rewire your reality accordingly.

Scientific Insight: The Epigenetic Code

When you shift your environment, emotions, and focus—your body releases new hormones that bind to cells and change your DNA.

That's real-time divine software updates.

Your thoughts are electric.

Your emotions are magnetic.

Your body is the manifestation machine.

Neuroscience shows that the subconscious mind processes information 500,000 times faster than the conscious mind. It runs most of your bodily systems automatically—including digestion, heart rate, immune responses, and even hormonal secretions tied to emotions.

According to Dr. Bruce Lipton, your subconscious was primarily formed between the ages of 0–7, and functions like a tape recorder—absorbing without filters. The field of epigenetics further proves that our thoughts, environment, and emotional states alter our gene expression and biology, meaning your SubC literally shapes your body and your destiny.

Universal Law: The Law of Mentalism

"All is mind; the Universe is Mental."

This Hermetic principle teaches that everything in creation starts as a thought. Since your SubC is the seat of repetitive thought, it becomes the engine behind your manifested reality. To change your life, you must change the mental images, beliefs, and energy patterns stored in the SubC.

Mastering the SubC

You are not here to be driven by old wounds. You are here to rewrite your inner code.

Reprogram your SubC by:

- Visualizing daily with vivid detail

- Speaking affirmations with emotional truth

- Breathing consciously to override automatic fear responses

- Feeling gratitude for what's coming as if it's already here

- Rehearsing your reactions so you're never caught off-guard

Train your inner child (SubC) with the love, clarity, and repetition it deserves. Show it the way home—to harmony.

Take the Driver's Seat

You are not here to be driven by unprocessed trauma or society's SubC. You are here to steer your vessel. The mind is the captain. The body is the ship. God is the wind, water, and stars guiding you home.

Welcome to the real game of creation: learning to code your life with breath, words, vision, and balance. You are no longer sitting at the kid's table. You are seated at the roundtable of conscious creators. So create like a God.

Journal Prompt:

What outdated SubC programs have been running in the background of your life? Where did they come from? Are you ready to overwrite them?

Affirmation:

"I guide my subconscious with love. I program it with vision. I speak life into my vessel. I am the captain of my soul."

Volume I – Chapter 3: The Mechanics of Manifestation

Section 18: We Are God Experiencing Itself

Subtitle: The Divine Feedback Loop of Creation

> "God is not some man in the sky. God is the 'I' behind your eye."

You are not separate from God. You are God—in form, in thought, in function. You are the creator walking inside its own creation. The experiencer and the experience. The artist and the art. The voice and the echo.

Every breath you take, every vision you hold, every word you speak is the quantum field expressing itself through you. That means your life isn't happening to you—it's happening through you, as you.

You are the Divine in drag, the Infinite in disguise.

You are the cosmic selfie of God.

DIVINE LOOP:

God creates → becomes creation → experiences itself through you → reawakens to itself → expands.

That's the Feedback Loop of Divinity.

You are the instrument, the observer, and the played note. 🎶

Scientific Insight:

Neuroscience shows that the brain cannot distinguish between imagined experience and physical experience. That's because consciousness is primary—not the body, not the environment.

In quantum physics, the observer affects the observed. The act of looking creates the outcome. That means you are both the player and the programmer.

You are not reacting to life—you are projecting it from within.

Universal Laws:

- Law of Divine Oneness – All is one; nothing is separate

- Law of Mentalism – The All is Mind; the Universe is mental

- Law of Correspondence – As within, so without

- Law of Perpetual Transmutation – Spirit becomes form, form returns to spirit

ORIGINAL EPIPHANIES FROM MY NOTES:

- "The Universe echoes my voice because I speak like God."

- "We are all just electrons connected to the same Atom. Big Bang. Entangled."

- "You or me? Really it's You, Me and the Sea. Will you see?"

- "God is the Wi-Fi. My knowing is the password."

- "We are the machine that doesn't know it's a machine."

WHY THIS MATTERS:

If you believed—truly knew—you were God in motion, what would you do differently?

Would you:

- Speak more intentionally?

- Think more lovingly?

- Breathe more purposefully?

- Treat your life as sacred, because it is your holy experiment?

Then do it.

God is watching—through your eyes.

Journal Prompt:

> "If I am God experiencing Itself, what am I here to create, heal, and feel through this version of me?"

Affirmation:

> "I am not separate from God. I am the eyes, the hands, the voice, the breath of God in action. I create with clarity, feel with divinity, and move with sacred power. I am God, experiencing joy, learning, and expansion—through me."

Volume I – Chapter 3: The Mechanics of Manifestation

Section 19: The Kingdom Within and the Kingdom Without

Subtitle: Reclaiming Dominion Over Your Reality- The King's Dome

> "You don't have to ask for something that's already yours."

The Kingdom of God isn't some far-off cloud palace.

It's within you—and all around you.

The Kingdom Within is the seat of your divine power.

The Kingdom Without is the reflection of your inner throne.

When you align your mind with truth, your outer world becomes your court.

Your thoughts command.

Your breath governs.

Your vibration legislates.

And your intentions decree.

> You were never meant to beg for blessings. You were designed to embody authority.

DOMINION = VIBRATIONAL SOVEREIGNTY

The moment you remember you are a God-being, you stop asking for crumbs and start activating your inheritance.

You don't have to "earn" worthiness.

You don't have to pray from lack.

You simply recognize that the Kingdom answers to kings and queens—and if you are of divine stock, then everything within the Kingdom is already encoded for you.

Scientific Insight:

The reticular activating system (RAS) in your brain filters what you see based on what you believe. When you believe something is yours, your subconscious starts finding paths to it—confirmation bias becomes your co-pilot.

Pair that with epigenetics—where belief affects biology—and you are literally coding your body and brain to match your divine expectation.

Universal Laws:

- Law of Divine Oneness – You are not separate from the Kingdom

- Law of Vibration – You must match the frequency of your inheritance

- Law of Correspondence – What is within will appear without

- Law of Assumption – When you assume dominion, manifestation obeys

Journal Prompts:

Where in my life have I forgotten that I am the heir, not the outsider?

Affirmation:

"I no longer ask for what is already mine. I am the Kingdom. I command with love, receive with faith, and live as divine royalty."

Volume I – Chapter 3: The Mechanics of Manifestation

Section 20: Paradigm is the Prism

Subtitle: Seeing Clearly Through the Soul's Correction

"People are living as fragments of fragments."

Your paradigm is your perception filter—and if the filter is stained, fractured, or foggy, then every experience gets distorted.

What most people call "reality" is actually a prism—bending the light of truth through unhealed trauma, inherited beliefs, shame, fear, comparison, and distraction.

Until the soul purifies the lens, you're not seeing clearly.

You're seeing your life through the broken glass of your past.

"Paradigm is the Prism." That's the whole game.

PERCEPTION CREATES EXPERIENCE

- If you believe people are against you, you'll find "proof."

- If you believe you're undeserving, you'll subconsciously block blessings.

- If you believe love is pain, you'll chase it in suffering.

And the cold part?

It'll feel real. But it's not truth—it's projection.

Scientific Insight:

Cognitive biases—like confirmation bias, negativity bias, and emotional reasoning—create mental shortcuts that alter how reality is interpreted.

When you do inner healing, these biases begin to unwind, and your perception becomes more aligned with what's really there, not just what your programming expects.

Universal Laws:

- Law of Mentalism – Your mind creates your world

- Law of Correspondence – Inner distortion = outer distortion

- Law of Polarity – The opposite is always available; choose another frame

- Law of Perpetual Transmutation – You can transmute perception by choice

NOTES OF TRUTH:

- "People are living as fragments of fragments."

- "You're not out of your mind, you're out of alignment."

- "Wake up, Sleeping Beauty. The spell is perception."

Journal Prompt:

What parts of my paradigm were built from pain? Am I ready to see life clearly, through the lens of my healed self?

Affirmation:

"I purify my lens and realign with truth. My soul sees clearly. My spirit chooses wholeness. I release the prism and walk in the light."

Volume I – Chapter 3: The Mechanics of Manifestation

Section 21: SPIRITUAL RESCUE EXIT STRATEGY- Trifecta

Subtitle: A Soul Mission Briefing for Liberation

When the teaching ends, the releasing begins.

Mission Briefing:

There comes a moment in every soul's journey when surviving isn't enough.

You're not here just to cope—you're here to command.

But first, you must break the spell of smallness.

This is your sacred system override.

The Spiritual Rescue Exit Strategy is a three-part liberation sequence for walking away from anything that:

- Confuses your path

- Contaminates your energy

- Or convinces you to stay beneath your power

This is not drama—it's deliverance.

Let's go.

1.

Sacred Permission: The Strength to Leave

"Some people love you just enough to keep you
small.
But not enough to see you free"

Before we heal, we must admit:

"This no longer serves me."

You do not owe your life to people who drain you.

You are allowed to evolve without their permission
slip.

You are allowed to say:

"I don't belong here anymore."

And you are not selfish for leaving. You are sacred for
saving yourself.

There comes a moment when your soul gets louder
than your excuses.

When your peace starts costing more than your pain.

When the little voice inside says:

"We can't stay here anymore."

This is that moment.

You Have Permission To:

- Leave the people who constantly misunderstand you

    No matter how long you've known them. No matter who they are.

- Stop explaining your boundaries to people who benefit from you having none

    You don't need to convince them. You need to release them.

- Walk away from roles that shrink you, gaslight you, or drain you

    Your role was never to hold everything together at the expense of yourself.

- Choose peace over performance. Clarity over chaos. Growth over guilt.

You were never meant to earn love by carrying the pain of others.

You were never designed to struggle for your worth.

They told you it was noble to stay.

But what's really noble is healing. Expanding. Creating a life that doesn't hurt to live in.

A New Normal Awaits:

In this new normal...

- You are not confused

- You are not blamed for feeling deeply

- You are not afraid to speak up

- You are not over-explaining your goodness

- You are not punished for your gifts

- You are not walking on eggshells around landmines called "love"

In this new normal...

You are safe. You are seen. You are supported.

Not sometimes. Not when they're in the mood. Always.

Remember:

You are not hard to love. You were just in a place where love was hard to find.

And baby, you deserve more than confusion disguised as connection.

You deserve:

- Joy without drama

- Support without shame

- Presence without performance

- Laughter without tension

- And love that doesn't feel like a chore

Final Affirmation:
I deserve to be free.
I deserve to be loved where I can breathe.
I release what drains me.
I accept what restores me.
I am not asking for too much.
I am just no longer settling for too little.
And I give myself full permission to begin again.

2.

"Get the F*ck On" Release Ritual

This is not a cute bubble bath and palo santo moment.
This is energetic eviction.

If it's draining your joy, your light, your focus, your magic—
It has to get the f*ck on.

Say it with your soul. This is your energetic eviction notice.

This ritual is about full-body clarity—cutting soul ties, pulling power cords, and walking out of spiritual contracts with dysfunction. It's not just about leaving them—it's about leaving the old version of you that tolerated them.

This ritual is a spiritual sword. Use it when you're done explaining, defending, hoping, or waiting for people to do right by you.

Some beings are not meant to evolve with you. Some energies only teach you how sacred your energy truly is.

You'll Need:

- 1 black candle (banishment + boundary)

- 1 white candle (purification + rebirth)

- A bowl of water or saltwater

- Pen + paper

- Fire-safe dish

- Your favorite crystal, blunt, or essential oil (optional)

- You, in your truth

Step-by-Step Ritual

1.

Set the Scene

Light your black candle and say:

> "I call back all energy that is mine.
> I release all energy that is not."

Take three deep breaths. Inhale clarity. Exhale foolishness.

2.

Write the Good-Bye Letter

On paper, write out everything you are releasing:

- Names of people, patterns, parasites

- Energies you tolerated but shouldn't have

- Old thoughts, outdated roles, identity illusions

Then say aloud:

> "These things no longer serve me. They are no longer mine.
> I thank them for the lesson. I release them from my field.

I am no longer bound. I am no longer fooled. I am no longer tired.
You had your chance. Get the f*ck on."

Burn the paper. Watch it turn to ash.

Or

Write their name, the habit, or the wound on a piece of paper.
Hold it.
Breathe in for 6 seconds.
Exhale for 6 seconds.
Say: "Thank you for the lesson. You may now GET THE F*CK ON."
Burn it, bury it, or flush it. The universe will handle the rest.

3.

Anoint and Affirm

Light the white candle and speak:

"I now fill the space I've cleared with truth, protection, clarity, and joy.
No more leeches. No more thieves. No more compromise.
This house (my body, mind, and soul) is under new management."

Dip fingers into water. Touch your third eye, heart, and crown.

4.

Seal the Shift

Say:

> "I walk forward untouched by the past.
> I am sovereign. I am sealed.
> No low vibration can sit at my table.
> I am no longer who I was when I allowed that.
> I rise. I fly. I shine. And it's permanent."

Blow out the black candle:

> "That chapter is closed."

Blow out the white candle:

> "This new era begins."

(Optional: Flip your middle finger toward the ash and say…)

> "Blessings on your journey. Just not in my direction."

Final Note to the Reader:

Repeat this ritual as often as needed.

Anytime your field gets foggy. Anytime you start shrinking again.

Anytime someone tries to sneak in the back door of your spirit with old keys.

You don't owe anyone a front-row seat to the version of you they never honored.

From this moment on... You are free.

3.

The Clean Slate Declaration: A Covenant With My Highest Self

Now that you've cleared the space, it's time to reclaim the throne.

This is where you write your new contract—not with fear, but with your divine self.

> Write this by hand, say it aloud, or repeat it until it roots:

CLEAN SLATE DECLARATION

———

Clean Slate Declaration: A Covenant With My Highest Self

I, Insert Your Name, declare this moment a holy reset.
Not because I'm starting over—
But because I'm starting aligned.

I am no longer available for:

- One-sided soul ties
- Energetic theft
- Conditional love
- Emotional breadcrumbs
- Spiritual misuse
- Silent competitions disguised as connection

I reclaim every piece of me that was overlooked, borrowed, or betrayed.

From this day forward:

I protect my power like the sacred technology it is.
I honor my mind as a vessel of divine intelligence.
I release guilt around outgrowing people who chose to misuse their access to me.
I let my fire fuel me, not consume me.
I speak my truth without apology—not because I'm angry, but because I'm clear.
I walk as the originator, not the imitation.
I no longer hand out access to priceless parts of me just because someone shows up hungry.

Let it be known:
My soul is no longer for sale. My light is no longer on clearance.

I am love. I am legacy. I am limitlessly reborn.

This is my Clean Slate.
This is my new agreement with the Universe.
And I step into it fully seen, fully heard, fully me.

Signed with sacred knowing,

_____

(Date)

I now declare that I am walking in my truth.

I cancel all contracts made in confusion.

I break ties with energy that no longer serves my soul's evolution.

I revoke access from all people, places, and patterns

that cannot rise with me.

I stand in my light, without shame, without guilt,

and without apology.

My past no longer governs my future.

My peace is sacred.

My energy is currency.

My body is a temple.

My life is a sanctuary.

And from this moment forward—I choose me.

> **Affirmation**:
> "I walk away clean. I rise on purpose. I am whole and I am free."

Final Note:

This isn't just a tool.

This is a template for transcendence.

Whenever you feel pulled back into the familiar hell of your past self—return to this ritual.

Repeat it.

Reclaim.

Reignite.

Because freedom is not a fantasy.

It's a frequency.

And baby, you just tuned in.

Volume I – Chapter 3: The Mechanics of Manifestation

Section 22: Spiritual Protection While Manifesting

Subtitle: Energetic Interference in a Yin-Yang Reality

"You don't just need vision—you need protection.

Because the moment you declare your light, darkness tries to negotiate your silence."

Teaching Section: The Reality of Resistance

When you begin manifesting consciously—aligning with your divine identity, visualizing abundance, speaking life—you become a vibrational disruption to everything that was built on your disempowerment.

The moment you shift into purpose, the resistance shows up.

Not because you're doing something wrong—

But because you're finally vibrating strong enough to be felt in unseen realms.

Just as there are forces aligned to uplift, activate, and support you…

There are also energies, entities, and even internal shadows that will try to block, delay, distract, or distort your frequency.

This is not fear-based thinking. This is spiritual awareness.

You must learn to manifest and defend.

To open portals of light while closing leaks in your field.

Because the battlefield isn't outside of you—it's energetic.

Universal Law – The Law of Polarity

This law states that for every force, there is an equal and opposite one.

Manifesting light will always stir shadow.

The key is not to fear it—but to fortify your frequency so it cannot touch you.

How to Stay Protected While Manifesting:

1. Clean your field before you cast your vision.

   (Clear clutter, detox, or do energetic smudging.)

2. Pray or affirm protection around your work.

   "No weapon formed against this

manifestation shall prosper."

3. Avoid leaking your vision to low-frequency people.

    Not everyone deserves early access to sacred plans.

4. Ground your manifestations with light rituals.

    Burn a candle. Wear protection crystals. Call in ancestors or guides.

5. Declare vibrational sovereignty.

    Say aloud: "Any energy not aligned with my divine mission must return to its source now. I am protected in all realms."

Scientific Insight: The Biofield & EMF Intrusion

The human body emits a measurable electromagnetic field. This biofield is sensitive to disruption—whether it's from emotional conflict, toxic people, digital overstimulation, or spiritual interference.

Protecting your vibration while manifesting is like sealing your electromagnetic frequency so you don't short-circuit your intentions.

Affirmation:

"I manifest in light. I am protected by light. I am aligned with forces that serve my highest timeline, and all interference dissolves in the presence of my divine will."

The 5D Shift & Dimensional Merge

Somewhere around 2011–2012, the energy on this planet began to quicken. Time began to feel accelerated, like it was slipping through our fingers faster each year. It wasn't just our perception — something changed. A prophet told me in 2011, "Life will change as we know it," and he repeated that phrase three times. Now I know why.

The Mayan calendar didn't signal the "end of the world" but the end of time as we knew it — a reset, a vibrational fork in the road. The old programs are dissolving. Around this time, people started experiencing the Mandela Effect, glitches in our collective memory that hint at timeline jumps or merging realities. And right alongside that, CERN's Large Hadron Collider was activated — not just exploring particles, but unknowingly (or knowingly) tearing the veil between dimensions, potentially.

Now, more people are seeing UFOs, spirit beings, and having spontaneous awakenings. The veil is thinning. Realities are bleeding into each other. Our 3D physical world is colliding with 5D consciousness, where time is nonlinear, creation is instant, and truth cannot be hidden.

This is the moment of integration — we are remembering that we are multidimensional. That's why all this is happening. We are waking up.

Original One-Bar Classics

Spoken Spells to Rewire Reality

> "It only takes one word to move a mountain—if it's spoken from God."

THE BARS:

- I don't chase, I choose.

- Energy is spiritual money—spend it like your soul depends on it.

- I don't attract what I want—I attract what I am.

- Be it until you see it.

- The future ain't waiting—it's vibrating.

- My breath is my yes. My exhale is my Ase'.

- God is the Wi-Fi. My knowing is the password.

- My Inner G creates my outer geometry.

- I said it. I meant it. I manifested it.

- Vibration first. Then matter.

- I'm not asking—I'm aligning.

- I got receipts. My manifestations are confirmed.

- Don't touch my radio dial—I'm locked on my frequency.

- The mirror is inside me. Life just reflects the vibe.

- This truth? It's ineffable. And baby, that means it can't be eff-ed with.

- I am God in action. I am the Inner G.

- I'm not predicting the future. I'm authoring it.

- Breath is the steering wheel. Spirit is the engine.

- I don't "wish." I will.

- I am the glitch in the matrix—and the code rewrite.

- I'm not following trends. I'm following Truth.

- I'm powered by Spirit and programmed for greatness.

- The tongue is the wand. Watch your spell work.

- I'm not just woke. I'm encoded.

- My destiny already knows my name. I just had to remember.

- I don't need permission—I have precision.

- My shadow doesn't scare me. We been dancing.

- The universe echoes my voice because I speak like God.

- Your thoughts are the trailer. Your life is the movie.

HOW TO USE:

- Speak one daily as a morning mantra

- Post them like coded breadcrumbs on socials

- Use them as chapter openers or journal prompt starters

- Print and post them around your home altar, mirror, or dashboard

- Text them to your future self

Manifestation Techniques: Everyday Divine Practices

1. Text Yourself Your Desires

   Turn your phone into a quantum tool—text your wishes, intentions, and affirmations to yourself. This physical action creates a vibrational imprint through words and technology, activating the ether and reinforcing intention.

2. Water Charging Pads & Rituals

   Use your handcrafted water charging jars or pads—infuse water with spoken blessings, affirmations, or poems. Speak your intention aloud while placing the water on your sacred pad. Drink the charged water to align your inner energy field with your manifestation.

3. Sing Your Desires

   Melody is vibration. Singing your goals—like a chant, mantra, or song—heightens emotion and imprints your desire deeper into the quantum field. Music activates the emotional and subconscious realm, amplifying the manifestation process.

4. Bedtime Meditation & Morning Rising Ritual

   Before Sleep: Visualize your future self, your desires already fulfilled. Let this be the last image your mind sees before drifting into theta state, the most powerful manifesting brainwave.

Upon Waking: Reaffirm your intention and greet the day with gratitude. This sets the frequency of your day and sends your vibration into high alignment immediately.

5. Write with Intent, Speak with Power

    Every written or spoken word is a seed. Keep a manifestation journal or sacred scroll. Write as if it is already done. Speak aloud as if you are narrating a completed reality.

6. Create Mini Rituals

    Whether lighting a candle, using your custom mirror or copper spiral device, or placing an intention under your pillow—ritual anchors spirit in physical form.

7. Feel, Don't Just Think

    Emotion is the energetic force in manifestation. Feel the joy, peace, and gratitude now as if you already have what you seek. This "emotional signature" is the code the universe responds to.

The Manifestation Equation

> "Reality is built by rhythm, encoded by emotion, and delivered through vibration."

FORMULA:

$$B + T + V(E) \times I = M$$

Where:

- B = Belief (faith without doubt/ knowing; the subconscious agreement that it is done)

- T = Thought (the image held clearly in the mind)

- V(E) = Vibration powered by Emotion (the frequency you hold, amplified by feeling)

- I = Intention (the focused, directed energy— desire with direction)

- M = Manifestation (the physical expression of your internal alignment)

Scientific Insight:

This mirrors epigenetics + quantum mechanics:

- Emotion affects the vibrational field, which alters cellular behavior (epigenetics).

- Focused intention affects probability waves, collapsing them into physical form (quantum field).

- Belief activates the reticular activating system (RAS), pulling matching evidence into awareness.

Universal Laws:

- Law of Vibration (Emotion is the fuel of frequency)

- Law of Mentalism (Thought is the blueprint)

- Law of Action (Focused intention sets movement)

- Law of Correspondence (Belief magnetizes outer match)

POETIC RESTATEMENT:

"What you believe + what you think + the feeling you fuel it with × the clarity of your command = the version of reality that responds to your vibration."

REINFORCED VERSION (with spiritual language):

(Breath + Belief) + (Vision + Voice) + (Vibration × Emotion) × Divine Intention = Manifested Matter

---

Poetic Spiritual Formulas for Manifestation

Formula 1: Electromagnetic Alchemy

> *Formula: E + T × I = M (Emotion + Thought × Intensity = Manifestation)*

Emotion is your energy in motion. Thought draws the blueprint. Intensity heats it up. When all three are aligned, the universe delivers.

Formula 2: What You Water, Grows

> *Formula: Attention + Repetition + Belief = Acceleration*

Every time you return to the frequency of your desire, it strengthens. Focus is your fertilizer.

Formula 3: Coherence Code

Formula: Mind + Heart =
Quantum Clarity

Your mind asks, your heart signs the check.
Coherence creates clarity in the quantum field.

Formula 4: Return on Intention (ROI)

Formula: Time + Energy +
Thought = Return

Whatever you invest in—fear or faith—you will
receive a return. The universe pays in kind.

Formula 5: Decision Activates the Delivery

Formula: Decision = Quantum
Command

Decision is spiritual law. Once you decide with clarity,
the universe rearranges itself to deliver.

Bonus Insight: The Spiral of Synchronicity

Formula: Aligned Intention +
Action = Evolution

Every moment of alignment spirals you higher. If the
result doesn't match, retune your frequency.

Volume I – Chapter 4: Metaphysical Memory –

Your Life as a Sacred Story

Volume I – Chapter 4: Metaphysical Memory – Your Life as a Sacred Story

Section 1: Life as a Divine Curriculum

Subtitle: You Weren't Meant to Forget

"You weren't meant to read this until you became the version of you that could interpret it. Now you're ready."

Your life is not a mess—it's a masterpiece in motion.

Every trial, trauma, delay, or detour was never punishment—it was preparation. Even the things that nearly broke you were tailor-made to build you. I've come to call this the Divine Curriculum—the custom soul syllabus you agreed to before birth. You didn't come to Earth school to suffer—you came to remember.

There's no wasted pain in this universe. Every heartbreak helped sand down your ego. Every disappointment recalibrated your direction. The breakup, the breakdown, the betrayal—they weren't barriers, they were breadcrumbs.

You weren't being delayed. You were being designed.

Universal Law: The Law of Divine Order
Nothing is random. Everything is unfolding according to divine alignment, even when it looks chaotic from the outside.

Scientific Insight:
Post-traumatic growth is a documented psychological phenomenon. Neuroplasticity allows new beliefs and behaviors to form through challenge and adaptation. You become stronger at the broken places.

Journal Prompt:

What has life taught me through pain, and how has that shaped the superpowers I now carry?

Affirmation:

I trust the curriculum of my life. Nothing was wasted. Every lesson became light.

Volume I – Chapter 4: Metaphysical Memory – Your Life as a Sacred Story

Section 2: The Memory Within the DNA

Subtitle: Uncoil Your Trauma

You are carrying more than just your own memories.

Inside your cells are echoes. Stories. Songs. Wounds. Triumphs. You are a walking archive of your ancestors' dreams and decisions. And even though you may not have lived their lives—you remember.

There was a moment when I felt something in my spirit I couldn't explain—a pull, a fear, a deep-rooted grief that didn't come from anything I had experienced in this life. That's when I realized: this wasn't just mine. I was carrying soul data passed down through the bloodline.

But here's the divine twist: what was passed down can also be healed.

Universal Law: The Law of Inheritance (Karmic & Energetic)
You inherit energy, not just genetics. But you also inherit the power to transform it.

Scientific Insight:
Epigenetics shows us that emotional trauma can alter gene expression and be passed to future generations. Conversely, healing and intentional practices like meditation, affirmations, and breathwork can

influence gene expression positively.

"Your blood is a USB drive full of stories you didn't live, but still remember."

Journal Prompt: What emotions or fears feel older than me—and what might they be asking me to transform?

Affirmation: I honor the memories within my DNA, and I choose to rewrite the patterns with love, clarity, and divine intention.

This Truth? It's Ineffable.

And Baby, That Means It Can't Be Eff-ed With.

"The highest truths aren't spoken—they're remembered."

Some things can't be explained—they can only be felt.

That's ineffable: too great, too sacred, too real to be reduced to words.

The truth of who you are—your divinity, your power, your cosmic assignment—can't be fully taught in a textbook or sermon. It hits your spirit like déjà vu. It stirs something ancient in your blood. It vibrates through the marrow of your being. It's a soul recognition, not a logical conclusion.

That's the realm of the ineffable.

And once you know it—you can't unknow it.

THE REVELATION:

When you say "I am God," it's not ego.

It's echo—the truth ringing back through time, space, and DNA.

This truth isn't just deep. It's dimensionless.

It lives beyond the tongue, beyond the brain, beyond the veil.

The moment you try to define it, it slips through the cracks of grammar—because it's not language, it's light.

And it's inside you.

Scientific Insight:

In quantum physics, the closer you get to measuring pure potential, the more it eludes capture. It behaves like energy and matter at once. The moment you observe it, it shifts.

That's the ineffable in motion: the divine cannot be boxed. It's everywhere and nowhere. It is being itself.

Just like consciousness. Just like God.

Universal Laws:

- Law of Divine Oneness – Truth is already encoded in you

- Law of Vibration – Truth is a frequency you feel, not facts you recite

- Law of Mentalism – What you think is limited; what you know is eternal

FROM MY ORIGINAL NOTES:

- "God is the 'I' behind your eye."

- "You don't chase the truth. It chases you. You just have to be still long enough to get caught."

- "Once you see, you can't unsee. That's the blessing and the burden of knowing."

Journal Prompt:

"What part of me already knows the truth, but has been waiting for permission to speak it?"

Affirmation:

"The truth of who I am cannot be erased, replaced, or debated. I am the living word. The embodied code. The ineffable revealed. And baby, that means I cannot be eff-ed with."

It vibrates beyond language.

And still—it's undeniable.

Untouchable.

Unfuckwithable.

Because it came from Source.

And Source don't play.

Casin' the Mason Joint

True Personal Experience

Every aspect of the world has positioned a mason in the forefront, spearheading a department, country, or company.

The mysterious and enigmatic Masons. The ones who make the world go round.

The upstanding citizens.

What if I told you they are not so much and I saw it with my own eyes.

Before the masses started to take notice that something was awry... in the government, with the entertainment industry, sports arenas, corporations, food and worst of all, education or should I dare say dead-you-cation.

The indoctrination of how to be a loyal follower. Follower of incompetent, careless, and uncompassionate authority figures, who aren't qualified to lead.

Followers of false doctrines put in place to keep us docile and complacent, which keeps us mentally sedated, so we never look up from our devices to notice the war going on around us.

The devices- cellular phones that break down our cellular structures, televisions that tell our vision lies, which both are labeled as smart so you will feel dumb if you don't have one, but it's really the devices that are dumbing us down.

Tablets are an instrument used to medicate and distract. Devices have turned into our vices that make us tamed followers, that never will see the light of our true potential.

A follower is a flower that never blossoms, better yet, it still is in its seed form waiting to be taken care of by the rain and sun.

Sometime in my past, back when I dated men, many eons ago, I used to date this guy that was a director at this university and he happened to be a mason. He was from Chicago and now was working in a rural college town in Bumfuckville midwest. I met him when some colleagues and I were hired to perform for a show.

What an amazing show it was. So much so, that me and the guy started a long distance relationship as a result of it.

We would talk on the phone to really get to know each other and he, at one point, came up to St. Louis to see me.

He was tall, dark and really handsome. He was super square and I was a classy chick from the hood, so I was well rounded.

I knew he had a hidden wild side when we went and got our nipples pierced. That right there, is another type of pain.

The type of pain that curls your toes, you immediately start sweating and shaking, then your vocal cords emit a sound frequency that you were unaware your body could even produce, but I digress.

So one weekend I made that 4 hour drive to see him. I was supposed to spend about a few days with him. That was the original plan but ya girl had to haul ass before the people " got me."

The first night he cooked for me, a full meal. Yum!

Sketched a beautiful picture of me, beginner locs and all. Yaaaaassss! Then invited me to a dinner at his masonic lodge for the next night.

A special night that you could bring your wife or girlfriend to. I was like OOOKKKAAAYYY. My black girl magic is working like a charm.

We may go to the next level of this relationship. He hit all the boxes on paper that the average black woman is looking for, so I thought.

Educated, Handsome, a Career, and a nice person that was open to having fun. So fast forward to the next day and we went to the mixer/ dinner at the lodge.

I was the only girlfriend there, everyone else was a wife- so in my head, I'm thinking that I'm very well on my way to consider the next step with him- even though I couldn't put my finger on what was amiss.

I thought it was the regular shmegular insecurities that sometimes come with having a long distance relationship.

From the random local chicks that may want a sample of chocolate, to the students that may shamelessly flirt because they are crushing on a man with power.

Little did I know, it was none of the above. Matter of fact any of those scenarios would have been better than the truth, because after that I looked at people, places and things differently. Basically all the nouns were ruined for me.

Let me paint a vivid picture to put things in context. We arrived at the lodge. I'm looking around at the majestic decor and surroundings, that put me in the mindframe of a cathedral or catholic church- which I am very familiar with because I was baptized and even went to catholic school and church, so that was the best reference point I had and it fit the bill.

The grandeur of it all. So he gave me a brief introduction to some of his lodge buddies and their wives. There was one wife in particular. We hit it off immediately.

We were talking, connecting, laughing and having a knee-slapping good time. As my date hung with his lodgemates, me and my new best friend chatted for about 45 minutes.

Then mid-sentence she looked to the left of us, then to the right. Stared directly in my eyes and asked me if I wanted to see something "cool".

Then in turn I looked to our left and then to the right and stared directly at her and said "Sure". So as the social was busy, we slipped away from the main room where the gathering was.

She led me down the hallway, around the corner, up the stairs and down a corridor. By this time, I'm thinking to myself, where is she leading me?

I'm wondering if she can tell that I'm into women and was gonna freak me down. Was she gonna tell my date because he definitely didn't know.

There were all kinds of thoughts that were going through my head. I wish it was just a simple case of bi-curious shenanigans. That would have been a lot funner than what was to come.

So we get midway down the corridor, then she stops and says "Do you want to see where the boys have their meetings??"

I was like "Yeah!" I was relieved there was no funny shit about to transpire because I really was trying to be on the straight and narrow. No pun intended.

So I'm standing there confused because we are in the middle of the hallway. She turns to the tan and brown wood panel wall, presses on it and I kid you not, a secret door popped open. I thought I was in a Bond movie but it wasn't Octopussy.

The door is open and the room is revealed, it was so clandestine. I entered the "chambers", as I really should call it.

The walls were painted ALL BLACK!

From the ceiling, the walls to the floor, and I'm not talking about Lil Jon and the East Side Boyz.

There were Pentagrams everywhere, along with skulls, fancy chalices and goblets that had RED residue in it.

Big ass black cloaks with hoods that hung to the floor. On the counter next to the chalices, there was a decorated handle, curved blade or "dagger" would be more accurate and next to it was a goat's head staring me in the face. Literally cloak and dagger. Now I know where that term came from.

This was in the late 90's, so I had no idea what to make of it all. My very first thought from my soul was "This is some Devil shit!."

I was walking around that joint like a person that's visiting someone's house that's filthy with roaches. I didn't want to lay a pinky finger on the air.

I was walking around examining everything closely, to wrap my mind around what I was looking at. I was thinking this can't be real.

Were these theater props? He didn't tell me he was an actor or in a play, I thought to myself.

The unnamed woman was studying my every movement, observing my reactions, probably to gauge my shock.

Everything gave me the heebee-geebees mixed with a sinking feeling in my gut. Right when my mind was officially blown. The woman said "I think it's time for us to go".

I concurred.

I made sure I didn't leave any evidence. No hair. No footprints. No heat signature.

So we swiftly headed to exit from the secret door. She carefully left out first and I followed behind.

As we made our way back down the corridor, down the steps and around the corner, I didn't say anything because I was officially freaked out.

She was saying something to me as we walked back but it all was background noise compared to my thoughts.

I'm thinking "What is this dude into?? What are all of these people, that are laughing, dancing and smiling, in that party into?? They all look so normal?!"

This building looks like a church, for heaven's sake.

Before my mind could come up with an answer, as soon as we hit the corner to come down the main hallway that leads back to the party, we were greeted by a group of at least 10 men with serious faces.

Walking our way and coming in hot. They approached us, firing questions at us. "Where were you all? Where did you go?"

Vanilla Sis came in clutch and filled right in with the storyline and the script.

She said "Oh, I was just showing her to the bathroom and the kitchen".. Blase, Blase.

I chimed in and was like "This is a lovely place, the artwork is fabulous! Magnifico!" or whatever the fuck I said because my mind was in a fog.

I felt like a tipsy person that sees the cherries in the rearview and has to sober up quickly to avoid jail. But in that moment my spirit said get it together, they are not gonna play with your black ass.

I didn't even see my date, he conveniently wasn't there for that part. He resurfaced after the fact and I faked the funk like I was having a wonderful time and stomached being there for however much longer.

 At that time I didn't know much about the Masons but they surely knew how to leave an impression. YouTube or social media wasn't a thing yet, mind you this is 1999 and I wasn't dreaming when I wrote this.

I had a permanent side-eye with him after that experience. I knew he was in the lodge by a thread. He was the only person of color in the club.

He came from a chapter in Chicago and once he moved, there was only one chapter in town. He joined and felt comfortable enough to stay because they must have similar practices at every lodge.

The Masons meet about the same things, in the same way- across the board. Like Mike said It don't matter if you're Black or White, the secrets and the agenda are the same.

I knew I had to plan my great escape. There was no way in hell I was staying in Devil-town with the spawn of Satan.

We went back to his place and I made an attempt to act normal even though my anxiety was building with a wide array of emotions and questions that I knew I would never ask.

 I'm sure he suspected but most likely was too scared to open that can of worms, better yet Pandora's box. We both were playing a game of cat and mouse but I wasn't going to get caught in that trap.

He tried to get frisky but I acted like I had "itis" from the under seasoned food at the mixer.

I laid awake that night, coming up with an excuse to cut this little visit short and get to a place where I felt safe. Back to the hood.

So cockadoodledoo, the early bird gets the worm and it wasn't coming out of that can.

I faked a call from my Ameritech cell phone. I said a bunch of Oh my God's, Nuh-uh's, WWWWWWHHHHAAATTT??!!'s and Really's.

I shook my head about 4 or 5 times and started gathering every single speck of belongings I brought there, for I knew this would be my last visit and most likely the last time I would EVER see him. I made that instant resolve when I was in the Dungeons and Dragons boys room.

He was asking me if I wanted to take any food that he made and asked am I sure I have to leave. Yes, I am positive and no thank you on the food, you can eat it.

When I say I skedaddled out of that door in an expeditious manner. I was tossing my suitcase in the back, talking fast and saying I had a great time and I will let you know when I make it back to the Lou. Adios and Sayonara.

I hopped up in my car so fast and pulled off with the quickness. I was checking my mirrors to make sure I wasn't being followed, by him or a mystery pick-up truck and what not.

I was checking my rearview for about an hour. I was shook.

I was thinking all kinds of thoughts but most of all, what would they have done to me if they caught us in the meeting room with all of their secrets that non-members are absolutely forbidden to see.

Now that I know so much more about them I pretty much have the answer as to what would have happened to me. I thought about why Vanilla Sis put me up on game.

It took about 10 years to figure that answer out. The wives of Masons have to go through their own secret keeping initiation with penalties for infractions.

Since I was just a girlfriend or in the dating stage, there still was time to save me. It seemed like she felt as if I wish someone would have told me what I was signing up for before I committed.

She knew I wasn't cut out for the ride that ol' boy was trying to take me on.

After I left, I spoke to the guy a few more times for good measure.

He asked about my emergency and how we need to have a do-over but I was conveniently unavailable for that part, just like he was at the party when those burly men came charging down the hallway looking like a tiki torch mob coming to get Frankenstein when the real monsters were them.

I made sure I was unavailable and kept it short when I did talk to him. After a while he told me he was getting back with his ex. I was thinking "Does she know that you into weird shit, but okay, good for y'all, congratulations, I guess."

He's more into Black Magic than Black Girls.

Fast forward some years later, when information is circulating and conspiracy theories are running wild. The higher ups are doing everything in their power to discredit, threaten, or do worse to people when they stand up for the truth to be exposed and the veil lifted with the curtain drawn.

I saw it with my own 2 eyes and was in the belly of the beast, uninitiated, and lived to tell the tale. I held on to this information, outside of a few close people, waiting on the right social climate to make it rain.

This needs to be in the open, so society can have a transparent view and accurate perception of who is running the place. Not just America but every nook and cranny is involved.

If they had this elaborate set up in Bumfuckville midwest, then it makes you wonder what kind of practices and meetings they are having at the corporate levels, the millionaire levels, the political levels, the music industry levels, the religious levels, and the educational levels.

The list can go on because it's definitely levels to this shit. That Red stuff in the chalice, I'm guessing was not Kool-aid.

PYROMANIAC

My purpose is to ignite fires and make you critically think

to free Minds of falsehoods that's got brains locked in the clink

and devour it as truth without any proof of its weight within a blink

Let others guide your fate like GPS with no satellite link

To lock our physical existence and minds in jail or some kind of prison.

And if you put up any type of resistance you're not a good Christian

or citizen or whatever it is that you believe in

Having your dreams of desires left unfulfilled along with the rest of the heathens

The Emptiness of going through the motions in in an emotionless Society, Non-Stop continuous cycle.

Ran by spiteful, frightful, no conscious having psychos.

Who can give a fuck about you, look what they did to Michael.

Erased him like a typo

And when they killed Prince, I've been in mourning ever since.

So ladies and gents, prepare yourself for an ILL Skillz presents.

Your feature presentation will cover all kinds of subjects from overblown budgets, to how they redirect our attention with funny ass memes of Muppets.

Sipping our tea and laughing at the inner me and why we love it.

Why everyones attitudes like 2 tears in a bucket and what of it..

The glass ceiling we live under so we see the sky but can't touch it.

So we can have wing envy and want to covet..

Jump on to Windows to fly but we plummet

When life pushes me down, I get up and shove it!

I have bigger dreams that burn in me like an oven.

I got million dollar ideas by the dozen and I hunger for it like a glutton.

Tryna make old money while I'm young, more Benjamin's than buttons.

I pray with the sage and Smudge it. Everyday for the dollars and duckets.

Well not everyday, The numbers, I fudged it.

But u get the jist of it. It's Definitely on my bucket.

Cuz you can't have a revolution without money and lots of it. Back on subject.

Time to project an audio film unto the masses

Unmask this covert regime of fascist that trash us

Global warming burning us up into ashes..Dust in the wind

Left out in the wild, wounded..how can we protect and defend

ourselves, offspring and kin

From wolves, bears, and grizzlies..

Elephants and donkeys is beyond me.

Honestly, the powers that be

will get you like green girls doing the prom thing

Totally fucked and sent packing.. No bus fare.

That's when it hits you that life ain't fair,

It's cold out there, and every nigga tryna get what's down there

beware of thugs and smiling strangers that stare..

It's a long walk home and you broke curfew.

I used this analogy to show how the man is shitting on you from a bird's view

in a private jet doing a number 2

On purpose to hurt you but disguise themselves as a person with virtue

But really they are a piece of poop covered in perfume.

I urge you to have discernment when it comes to the people you let in your circle.

Because the same people that you let inside will be the same ones that curse you.

Hindsight is 20/20, I've got to say plenty until my mind is empty on it.

Spill the beans until I verbally vomit

and Purge until there's a surge of power from the ones it shorted.

Yes black lives matter but as soon as white money gets involved missions get aborted

They come in like made men and made men Bend to their will.. contorted

then distorted the message, broke the compass, lost Direction on our path. Just look at our past and TRULY report it

All of our organizations that pose a threat to white supremacy get thwarted

Spied on, then infiltrated by enemies that become right hands who go left,

become heads and hold chairs and dares anyone to come for their necks.

Tear down the infrastructure and leave it to the janitors to clean up the mess while they take the checks.

It is the Kansas City Shuffle at best.

It happens cuz black folks be so quick to impress,

invite others to have free range of our culture and struggles like be my guest.

Make yourself at home, kick your feet up, get some rest.

Raid the fridge of my fruits, I made sure they are fresh.

Pull up a seat at my table, I don't have much.. Do you like it? Please say yes.

But let the tables turn and you're the one trying to get a seat where they meet

You think you just gonna walk up, knock on the door, come in and wipe your feet, have a seat and let's eat.

Pass the peas. So many smiles and cheese, Being here is such a treat.

But in reality it's more like look who's coming to dinner,

but its even bigger cuz as soon as you step a toe on their property

they turn on the sprinklers, call the police, all while they are cocking the

shotgun standing their ground with laws backing them to the point they know no one is stopping me

and it's not probably but they will get off, won't even have to cop a plea.

The Oddity of those two different outcomes, honestly

We historically play into the hands of our dealer.

We've become so predictable at this point they know we will search for our own killer.

Give him all of the keys to the castle then befriend him and make him familiar.

Such an intricate part of your existence till he's head of your Familia,

but he's more like that creepy uncle that touched all the kids in a secret way

when he took them to that pizza place

with John and Tony, Pizzagate

It's a shame higher ups are treated as special,

Hollywood and politics is run by some Pedos!

Makes me want to pull out my metal,

a gun or blade and just let go on the sickos

They do it all under our big nose.

Do you smell what my spirit is cooking??

But not the kind Marina is doing with all of your faves booking

Satanic celebs, protected by the feds, cauldron and all

In bed with the politicians plus a few voodoo dolls.

A GAJILLION reptilians on television screens

But we soo focused on the wrong green, the wrong thing.

Secret societies Ain't So secret no more.

We've blown the hinges off those doors

and for those who choose not to come in and see what's behind it all. Keep blinders on,

Choose to keep pretending

To see the Grand Wizard of Oz is just a man behind the machine controlling us with lies since the beginning .

especially those with melanin

Ted Turner said that they will decrease the population by 80%, minimum

Who do you think they are going to start with? I keep telling them.

But it's easier to fool people than to convince them they've been fooled quotes from Mark Twain,

In order for some to get it I would have to say it again.

But they won't hear me cuz they are too busy praying, I'm just saying.

Leading the Sheep to the Wolves to get slain.

We must change the Collective Consciousness even if we have to sever the brain.

Of this train of thought, the game is bought not taught.

We're running face-first into the onslaught of our people .

The game is so evident it's see through

from music magic, to mass incarceration,

to relationship destruction to carcinogen medication,

to fluoride in our water supply

to blind our third eye once it calcifies.

To unarmed black men getting murdered right before our eyes

and you can stream it in real-time cuz they went live. Then scroll it

and watch Kermit and Miss Piggy say all the things we want to say but can't own it.

Cyber friends with our enemies just so we can lurk and stroll it.

ADD to STDs, a compulsive nature that we don't even try to control it.

Posting your soul for free and you have no idea you've already sold it

To those that have the mentality that they need a job in order to get paid.

To be under the wing of The Man, He's Got The Whole World In His Hand and comfortably under his bosom you lay .

Complacent and oblivious to the reality that's plain to see

The dope is laced with anthrax to zombie shit. A to Z.

The illusion of Independence, and false sense of security just waiting for the rug to get pulled from under your feet.

But I'm laying the game out for all of us to see.

Immerse yourself in the reality that all we got is just you and me. Black Wall Street.

If I have to burn it all down, for some better flowers to grow

I'll be a Pyromaniac everywhere this message flows, shows and goes

We gotta pay the cost together, that's the only true way we can be free.

This concludes my audio film. Please press repeat.

ILL Skillz 4/12/2017

The difference between us, as a people, and many other groups is this: We were deliberately stripped of our indigenous culture. While others were allowed to practice, preserve, and remember who they were—we were forced to forget. We were made to create something different… something fragmented… a survival-based remix of a once-whole spiritual essence.

Volume I – Chapter 5: The Grand Scheme of Sound –

Spells, Symbols & the Sonic Self

Volume I – Chapter 5: The Grand Scheme of Sound – Spells, Symbols & the Sonic Self

Section 1: Sound Healing & DNA Upgrade

Subtitle: Recalibrating the Code with Frequency and Intention

"This wasn't a spa day. This was a soul command. I didn't learn it from a healer — God whispered it through the bowl. I just followed the sound and remembered I was made of music."

I didn't go looking for sound healing—it found me.

One day, I was at home, minding my own divine business, when I felt the nudge. Not from a person, not from a podcast, but straight from God. I had a singing bowl nearby—probably decorative, maybe intuitive—but something said, "Pick it up. Put it on your body."

Not beside me. On me.

Now mind you, I had never seen anyone do that before. This wasn't some YouTube tutorial. It was pure divine direction. The voice was clear: "Place it here." First my chest. Then my stomach. Then the parts of my body that held old emotions, tightness, memories.

Each time I struck the bowl, something unlocked. Not just on the surface—deep. The vibrations didn't just echo—they entered. I could feel my cells responding. My DNA stretching like it was waking from a nap. It was as if the sound was reading me like Braille— decoding and reorganizing everything I didn't know had been scrambled.

I lay there tingling, stunned, remembered. That sound didn't come from outside of me—it came through me. Like the bowl was God's stethoscope and tuning fork at once. And my body? A symphony that had been waiting to be reawakened.

What Is Sound Healing?

Sound healing is the sacred use of intentional frequencies to restore harmony to the body, mind, and spirit. Whether it's bowls, tuning forks, gongs, or your own voice—sound creates structure. And structure is the framework of reality.

Science calls this cymatics: the study of how sound moves through matter to create shape. The higher the frequency, the more beautiful and complex the form. So when you place a vibrating bowl on your body—especially since your body is over 70% water—you're not just hearing sound. You're sculpting yourself with sacred frequency.

I didn't need a scientist to tell me it was working. My nervous system relaxed. My thoughts slowed. My emotions softened. I felt it. My spirit understood every note.

Scientific Insight: Vibrational Medicine & Water Memory

- Your cells and organs resonate at unique frequencies. When they're out of tune, it shows up as stress or illness. Sound brings coherence—like tuning an instrument.

- Water stores memory. Your body is mostly water, which means sound doesn't just pass through—it informs, reprograms, and heals.

- Some studies suggest sound can influence DNA. Whether science has caught up yet or not, I knew in my spirit: my code was being rewritten.

Universal Law: The Law of Resonance

You don't attract what you want. You attract what you resonate with. Sound healing aligns your vibration with your intention. You're not just listening—you're tuning. You're reminding your body of the frequency it was born to carry.

Try This: At-Home Sound Healing Ritual

You'll need:

- A singing bowl, tuning fork, or your own humming voice

- A quiet space

- A glass of water (optional)

Steps:

1. Set a clear intention. Ask your body what's asking to be healed or harmonized.

2. Place the bowl or tuning fork directly on the area you're called to. If using your voice, rest your hand there and hum gently.

3. Strike or sound the bowl. Feel it ripple through your body.

4. Breathe deep. Inhale through your nose, exhale through your mouth. Anchor the frequency.

5. Stay in stillness and whisper:

   "I receive this frequency. I remember who I am."

6. Sip the water slowly. Let it ground the shift.

Journal Prompt:

What part of your body or spirit has been trying to speak to you lately? What would it sound like? Where does the vibration need to land?

Affirmation:

I am attuned to the divine song within me. Every cell listens, every organ harmonizes. I remember my original sound—and it is holy.

Volume I – Chapter 5: The Grand Scheme of Sound – Spells, Symbols & the Sonic Self

Section 2: The Sonic Blueprint – How Sound Shapes Reality

Subtitle: Exploring cymatics and sacred geometry

"The Universe didn't begin with a bang. It began with a sound. And every sound since has shaped the form of the formless."

Before I understood the science, I felt the truth.

Late nights in stillness… early mornings filled with birdsong… even the subtle hum of my own breath—I could sense something intelligent in the air. It wasn't just sound. It was structure. A language without letters. A blueprint in motion.

One day, mid-reflection, the revelation dropped:

What if sound is the blueprint of everything we see?

That thought hit me like thunder. And just like always, when a divine download lands, confirmation isn't far behind.

I began to randomly—but divinely—encounter cymatics videos, sacred chants, and ancient sound rituals. One clip showed grains of sand on a metal plate forming perfect geometric patterns when exposed to certain frequencies. The higher the tone, the more beautiful the shape.

That wasn't just vibration. That was instruction.

Sound was shaping reality in real-time. Not just externally, but internally. And suddenly, everything made sense—from the chants of monks to the way certain songs bring tears, to why we say "speak it into existence." Because you're not just speaking. You're shaping.

Universal Law: The Law of Vibration

Everything in the universe vibrates. Nothing is ever truly still. Every thought, word, and action emits a frequency—and that frequency becomes an instruction manual for how reality unfolds around you.

Your voice is vibration.

Your emotions are vibration.

Your intention is vibration.

And vibration is how matter knows what to become.

This is why sound carries so much power in spiritual practice. Why mantras are chanted aloud. Why affirmations work better when spoken with feeling.

Because sound organizes energy. Sound tells matter what shape to take. In short?

Sound is a spell.

Scientific Insight: Cymatics & Sonic Geometry

Cymatics is the visual study of sound in action. In these experiments, sound is played through metal or glass surfaces covered with fine particles like sand or salt. Each frequency rearranges the particles into unique, symmetrical patterns—proof that sound physically reshapes reality.

- Low, chaotic tones = jagged, unstable shapes

- High, harmonious tones = beautiful, geometric precision

So what does this mean for your life?

It means your body, your space, and your future are all listening to the sound of your frequency. And what you chant, sing, affirm, or say—becomes form.

Quick Ritual: The 5-Minute Sonic Reset

You'll need: Just your voice and your breath

Steps:

1. Sit or stand still. Close your eyes. Inhale deeply three times.

2. Place your hand over your heart. Say your own name out loud—slowly and intentionally.

3. Say this aloud:
   "I am a divine conductor of sound. My words shape worlds."

4. Chant "OM" or "AHH" for a full breath. Feel the vibration echo in your chest and skull.

5. Visualize the sound expanding like ripples— through your body, your room, and the world beyond.

Repeat daily or whenever your energy feels off. You are your own tuning fork.

Journal Prompt:

What sounds have shaped your life the most—words from others, music, your own voice? What do you need to start saying to yourself, out loud?

Affirmation:

My voice is a tuning fork for miracles. I speak with harmony, and the universe echoes back with form.

Volume I – Chapter 5: The Grand Scheme of Sound – Spells, Symbols & the Sonic Self

Section 3: Word Spells – Phonetics, Spelling, and the Language of Manifestation

Subtitle: Writing our reality one word at a time.

"Every time you speak, you cast a spell—just ask the ones who taught you to spell words."

Words are not just how we communicate—they're how we create.

Somewhere along the way, we forgot that. But I didn't. Not completely. Even as a child, I sensed it. Words carried weight. There were certain phrases I'd hear, and they'd stick to me—not just in meaning, but in energy. Later in life, that awareness returned like a divine reminder:

They call it spelling for a reason.

Spell. Spelling. Spelled.

You're not just expressing. You're casting.

Every time you speak, you're laying down a blueprint. Every word becomes an instruction to the quantum field. The question is: are you cursing your life unconsciously—or blessing it with intention?

Because the Universe isn't listening to your grammar. It's responding to your vibration.

We've been conditioned to speak carelessly:

- "I'm broke."

- "I'm dead."

- "This is killing me."

We say these things casually, unaware that our bodies, minds, and surroundings are taking them literally. The ancients knew. The mystics knew. Even today's marketers know: Repetition, rhythm, and sound = influence.

And the real magic? It's not just in what you say—it's in how you say it.

The frequency behind your voice. The phonetics of your spell.

Universal Law: The Law of Vibration + The Law of Cause & Effect

Every word is a cause.

Every result is an effect.

If your words carry vibration—and vibration moves matter—then your words literally create your world.

Your sound = your spell.

Energetic Wordplay Examples:

- Cursive = Curses — What are you writing into your life?

- Write / Right / Rite — Are you expressing? Correcting? Performing a sacred ritual?

- Spelling = Spell-ing — Every sentence is a ceremony

- Manifest = Mani + Fest — A hand (mani) celebration or creation

- Morning = Mourning — What are we grieving every day we rise?

These aren't just linguistic quirks. These are metaphysical breadcrumbs.

The subconscious doesn't just understand language— it feels it. That's why kids learn through song. That's why incantations, affirmations, and mantras work. Not because of semantics—but sound mechanics.

Quick Ritual: Rewriting the Word Code

1. Choose 3 phrases you say often (e.g., "I'm tired," "I can't," "I'm trying")

2. Rewrite each one with power. Example:

- "I'm resting and recharging."

- "I'm rising and reclaiming."

- "I'm in motion and aligned."

3. Say each new phrase out loud three times while standing in a power stance.

Let your voice reprogram your field.

Journal Prompt:

What phrases are you ready to retire? What words do you want to start speaking into your life?

Affirmation:

I speak with divine intention. My words are spells of truth, power, and creation.

Volume I – Chapter 5: The Grand Scheme of Sound – Spells, Symbols & the Sonic Self

Section 4: The Alphabet of the Body – The Letters We Wear in Flesh

Subtitle: Decoding the hidden language in our anatomy

"Your body is a book written in the alphabet of God. Every part of you is a letter—alive, breathing, and encoded."

This hit me out of nowhere—one of those stop-everything kind of revelations.

I was sitting, reflecting on how letters form words and words shape worlds, when suddenly I looked at my own body… and it hit me: We're wearing the alphabet.

Our physical forms are made up of symbols. Shapes. Sacred geometry in flesh. And not just randomly—but divinely aligned with the very letters we use to spell our realities.

Think about it:

- A is for Arm — angular, extended, shaped like the letter when raised or outstretched

- L is for Leg — especially when bent or resting, your leg forms an unmistakable "L"

- S is for Spine — curved and serpentine like the sacred letter

- B is for Breast or Butt — twin curves, looping just like the capital B

- e is for Ear — curled inward, like a lowercase e

- I is for Eyes — a pair of dots, like dotted i's- phonetically speaking

- N is for Nose — the shape and protrusion from the face

- T is for Torso — the central column with arms outstretched, like a cross

- V is for Vagina — the positioning between the thighs creates a V shape

Once you see it, you can't unsee it. There are many more examples once you think about it.

I realized we're not just speaking spells—we're spelled into being.

We're literally written in form. Walking, breathing sigils of creation.

Scientific Insight: Sound Forms Matter

In cymatics, when sound frequencies are played through a surface (like water, sand, or metal), they don't make random shapes. They form letters, symbols, and intricate geometry. Sound = structure.

If sound can organize sand, it can organize flesh.

And if your body was formed in a sound-based universe, then of course your form carries frequency—and code.

Universal Law: The Law of Correspondence

As above, so below. As within, so without.

Your body reflects the vibration of your soul—and the structure of the cosmos. Each letter your body mirrors corresponds to a truth you were born to live out. You're not just a person. You're a living word of the Divine.

Personal Reflection:

After this download landed, I looked in the mirror differently. Not in vanity. In reverence. I traced the curve of my spine. The bend in my elbow. The length of my legs. I whispered aloud, "I am spelled by God." And in that moment, I wasn't thinking about flaws. I was thinking about function.

Sacred symbols don't have to be perfect. They just have to be activated.

Ritual: Body Letter Activation

You'll need:

- A mirror

- Quiet space

- (Optional) a marker to trace letters gently on your skin

Steps:

1. Stand in front of a mirror with full presence

2. Choose 3–5 body parts and say their name aloud (e.g., "Arm")

3. Move or trace your body into the shape of that letter

4. Say:
   "I acknowledge this part of me as a sacred letter in the language of creation."

5. When finished, close with:
   "I am the alphabet of God in motion."

This isn't just self-love—it's soul literacy.

Journal Prompt:

What part of your body have you ignored, shamed, or overlooked? How might seeing it as divine language help you love it more?

Affirmation:

My body is the alphabet of the Divine. Every curve, every angle, every shape is a sacred syllable spelling out my purpose.

Volume I – Chapter 5: The Grand Scheme of Sound – Spells, Symbols & the Sonic Self

Section 5: Texting the Universe – Emojis, Glyphs & Spiritual Coding

Subtitle: Revealing the power of digital hieroglyphs, symbolic messages, and how texting is spellwork in disguise.

"Symbols speak louder than words—because they bypass language and go straight to the soul."

I didn't realize what I was doing at first.

I'd send strings of emojis under posts. Add a little sparkle, a flame, a lightning bolt. Sometimes, words didn't feel like enough. But every time I hit send, something inside me tingled. I wasn't just communicating—I was casting.

That's when the realization hit:

Emojis are modern glyphs.

We're not just texting for fun—we're texting the field.

You ever sent a text out loud in your head before you hit send?

You weren't just thinking—you were transmitting.

You ever dropped a heart emoji on someone's message and felt like that said it all?

You weren't just reacting—you were coding.

And guess what? You've been texting the Universe this whole time.

Every phrase, every emoji, every voice note dripping with emotion—that's a broadcast. And the Universe isn't waiting for perfect grammar or long-winded prayers. It's responding to frequency, tone, and intent. You are speaking in vibration, even when you think you're "just typing."

So when you say things like "I'm dead 💀" or "FML," or even "I'll never get out of this," those are spells.

When you say "I'm blessed ✨," "Money flows to me 💰🪙," or "Thank you, more please 🙏💫"—you just placed an energetic order.

Your energy is the ink, and your emotion is the signature.

Growing up, I was always drawn to symbols. Hieroglyphs. Dreamcatchers. Stained glass windows. Even tattoos. I didn't have the words for it then, but my soul remembered.

Symbols collapse feeling into form.

They don't require translation. They carry energy.

And they've always been used to communicate with Spirit.

Now we do it with phones.

A laughing face. A crown. A shooting star. These are offerings. Vibrational signals. Modern-day sigils. When used intentionally, they become prayers with pixels.

Because let's be honest:

The Universe doesn't respond to perfect grammar.

It responds to vibration.

Personal Epiphany

There was a moment I realized I was texting everyone else my thoughts but hadn't texted the Universe directly. So I started writing little notes to God. Sometimes with emojis. Sometimes in shorthand. But always in feeling.

And you know what? I started seeing things shift.

Not because I wrote a perfect spell—

But because my soul meant it.

Now I send messages to the Most High like,

"Thank you for the overflow 🏦 🎯 💎 ✨ I receive it with joy." or

"Client paid early 🕺 Grateful and aligned." or

"More peace, more sleep, more softness 💚 🕊️ 🪶 —
thank you in advance."

And I visualize the Divine opening the message like,
"Bet. Order confirmed."

Scientific Insight: Symbol Recognition, Neural
Encoding & Digital Spellcasting

Modern neuroscience confirms that the human brain
processes symbols and images far faster and more
powerfully than words. This is known as pictographic
cognition—a primal function that predates written
language. The visual cortex and limbic system instantly
interpret symbols, triggering emotional and
physiological responses without conscious decoding.

When you send an emoji—be it 💚, ⊙, or 🪔—
you're engaging in neurolinguistic programming via
imagery.

This activates:

- Mirror neurons (empathy and reflection)

- Emotional memory (associative recall)

- And even neurochemical release (dopamine,
  oxytocin, cortisol)

These tiny digital glyphs become vibrational shortcuts, imprinting intentions directly into the recipient's subconscious—like modern sigils.

Just like ancient hieroglyphs or cave paintings, emojis and symbols today carry layered meanings, becoming energetic keys that can unlock joy, pain, safety, desire, or power.

In quantum terms:

Every digital message is a frequency packet.

Every text is a transmission.

When you "text the Universe" using symbols, affirmations, or emojis—your digital spell becomes a vibrational petition encoded with intention, image, and energy.

Universal Law:

Every word you speak, type, or think carries a frequency. The Universe picks up on the feeling tone, not the format. Your intent is the engine. Your vibration is the GPS. And your language is the steering wheel.

If you're unclear in your message, your manifestation wanders.

But when you get bold and intentional—even in a tweet or a group chat—the quantum field gets the memo.

Ritual: Text Your Desire Into the Quantum Field

Do this when you need a quick alignment or want to practice active manifestation.

What You'll Need:

- Your phone (or a pen + paper)

- A quiet moment of clarity

- Optional: a favorite emoji you associate with your dream

Steps:

1. Open a new message to yourself or your Notes app.

2. Type or write your desire like you're texting a trusted friend:

   "Thank you for my new home 🏠 🌀 It feels peaceful, safe, and aligned with me."

   OR

   "I'm so grateful for divine timing. My partner and I are deeply in sync 💝 🔥 🙏"

3. Hit "send" or simply close the note, knowing the frequency has been transmitted.

4. Optional: screenshot it and revisit it later to feel the vibration again.

Esoteric Insight: Vibration Over Syntax

The Universe doesn't care how eloquent your sentences are—it cares about how you feel when you type them.

That's why tone, visuals, and repetition matter more than phrasing.

It's also why emojis, glyphs, and symbols carry so much metaphysical weight. They skip the logic center and hit the subconscious—direct access to Source.

Try This: Text a Desire into the Field

1. Open your notes app or a journal

2. Use only emojis to represent something you're calling in

   ○ Example: 😺 🎇 ⚜ 🌍 ☑

   (Translation: Sovereignty. Wealth.

Peace. Global reach. Elevation.)

3. Say it out loud like a coded prayer

4. Close your eyes. Feel it land in your body.

That's not just manifestation.

That's digital spellcasting.

Journal Prompt: Which emojis or symbols do you naturally gravitate toward—and what do they really represent to you? What symbols are part of your soul's signature? If the Universe scrolled through your recent thoughts like a text thread, what messages would it be responding to?

Affirmation: I speak to the divine in every language— especially the ones without words.

"My words are codes. My emotions are keys. I text the Universe in vibration, and it always texts back in divine alignment."

Volume I – Chapter 5: The Grand Scheme of Sound – Spells, Symbols & the Sonic Self

Section 6: Sound as Technology – Ancient Tools & Modern Frequencies

Subtitle: Keeping Your Vessel Tuned For Divinity

"What we call music today, they once called medicine."

> Long before we had words for "frequency" or "resonance," the ancients knew: sound was a tool of creation. Across every civilization, sound wasn't simply expression—it was technology. It opened doors, healed bodies, activated memory, and communicated with the Divine. Today, science is just beginning to confirm what our ancestors already knew: sound shapes reality.

Cymatics is the study of visible sound and vibration. When sound frequencies pass through a medium—like water, sand, or salt—they create geometric patterns. The higher the frequency, the more complex the pattern. These are not random designs. These are the language of creation, the blueprints of form.

In essence, cymatics is proof that sound creates matter. That our world is literally molded by frequency.

This is spiritual technology.

Not decoration. Not vibe. Not performance.

A tool. A system. A transmission line between Spirit and Self.

Scientific Insight: Cymatics & Bio-Tuning

- Cymatics shows how sound organizes matter—forming sacred geometry in sand, salt, or water

- Your body is over 70% water, making it the perfect sound conductor

- Frequencies like 432 Hz and 528 Hz have been studied for their potential healing effects on DNA, cellular repair, and nervous system balance

Ancient civilizations already knew:

- Egypt used sistrums

- India used mantra

- Australia used the didgeridoo

- West Africa used drum rhythms for emotional release and portal activation

This isn't new. It's just remembered.

Universal Law: The Law of Frequency Alignment

You don't just heal with knowledge—you heal with vibrational contact. When your body encounters a healing frequency, it doesn't need to "understand" it—it just responds.

That's why this technology works whether you believe in it or not. It bypasses your mind and tunes your field.

At-Home Ritual: Vibrational Reset

You'll need:

- A singing bowl, tuning fork, or sound app

- A quiet space

- Your body as receiver

Steps:

1. Choose a spot on your body that feels tense, heavy, or energetically blocked

2. Rest your tool gently on that area

3. Strike, hum, or play the tone

4. Close your eyes and breathe. Let the vibration move through your body like a wave

5. Whisper:

    "I remember this frequency. I remember myself."

Let the sound be your tuning fork, not just for health—but for wholeness.

Journal Prompt:

What tones, songs, or sounds have shifted you— brought you to tears, brought you home, brought you back to life? Could that be your original resonance returning?

Affirmation:

I am a tuning fork of God. My body remembers every sacred song.

Volume I – Chapter 5: The Grand Scheme of Sound – Spells, Symbols & the Sonic Self

Section 7: Chants, Mudras & Power Poses – Locking in Vibrational Commands

Subtitle: Tools for Quantum Anchoring

"You don't have to raise your voice to command power—just your frequency."

Sometimes, I forget how powerful I really am.

Not because I'm weak—but because I'm human. Because the world conditions us to shrink, to "stay humble," to wait for permission. But then it happens…

I speak something with conviction, and my entire nervous system shifts.

I lift my arms in a V like I already won—and my whole frequency clicks.

I hum while praying, and my crown tingles like a switch just flipped.

That's not random. That's ritual.

I used to think power was loud.

But now I know—it's vibrational.

Years ago I read a study about power posing—how just two minutes of standing in a confident stance could lower cortisol and increase testosterone. But that wasn't the whole truth.

What that study missed is this:

These aren't new discoveries. They're ancient body codes.

- A raised hand isn't just a stretch—it's a sigil of command

- A bowed head isn't just surrender—it's submission to Source

- A mudra isn't a finger pose—it's an energetic lock

Your body is already speaking... the question is: Are you listening to what it's saying?

Mudras & Power Poses: Unlocking Divine Circuits

- Gyan Mudra (thumb + index): Wisdom, clarity

- Abhaya Mudra (palm outward): Fearlessness and protection

- Victory Pose (arms raised in a V): Expansion, confidence, energetic arrival

- Heart Hands: Love transmission

- Prayer Hands: Alignment and balance

These aren't aesthetics—they're ancient programming keys.

When you pose, your spirit speaks louder than your words.

Chanting = Frequency in Motion

When you chant or hum:

- You align breath, vibration, and intention

- You activate the vagus nerve (which governs your parasympathetic nervous system—aka peace, rest, and intuition)

- You broadcast your energy as wave not just word

That's why "OM" calms the storm. Why singing lifts sadness. Why crying with sound brings relief.

You are the speaker and the spell.

Ritual: Embodied Declaration

You'll need: A mirror and your voice

Steps:

1. Stand in front of the mirror

2. Raise your arms in a V shape—like you just won a battle (because you did)

3. Look yourself in the eyes and say:

   "I command divine alignment. I am the embodiment of God-power."

4. Repeat it three times—louder each time

5. Watch what happens in your face, your eyes, your spine

6. Whisper:

   "It is done."

That's not just affirming—that's coding your frequency.

Journal Prompt:

What pose or movement makes you feel most divine? How can you incorporate it into your daily spiritual routine?

Affirmation:

I am a living sigil. My voice, my hands, my stance—all radiate divine instruction.

Energy vortex

Sound healing
cymatics

The Frequency Thief   WiFi analogy   Mental gardener

Gaslights, Cameras, Distraction-True

Personal Story

Before the days of social media, when the struggle was extremely real to get seen and heard, I managed to get my feet in the door. Back in 1999 or 2000 I just finished my first musical project, solo debut album, Tha Locs.

It was my beautiful brain child. I poured my heart and soul into it. It varied from spoken word to soul to rock.

I got some recognition from local newspapers and magazines and it gained momentum. There were a few articles written about it and I was shopping my project around to places, wanting to maximize my opportunities.

It felt like my hard work was paying off and I would at last see the fruits of my labor. I made it out of the poetry club to my BIG meeting. Finally!! My talent would be recognized. The meeting that could change my life. All the bullshit I had to crawl through was going to be rewarded.

So I thought.

I landed a meeting in LA with an industry insider that was full of connections. I garnered the attention of a record exec named Ira. He was a really tall, Jewish guy with dark curly, shoulder length hair, sturdy build but not flabby. He heard my CD and loved it!

He wanted to talk business to see how we can take it to the next level. So with that being said, I hustled up a way to get to Los Angeles from St. Louis to have my big meeting that was potentially my gamechanger.

To say I was super excited was an understatement. I almost passed out every time I even thought about it.

Just so happened that a friend, who worked in the same salon as me, had a homegirl that needed to go to LA to check on her apartment in Burbank and go to traffic court. She performed in music videos and was somewhat of a Latina video vixen.

All 3 of us were going to drive down together but at the last minute my friend canceled, but me and her homegirl still had shit to handle, so the show must go on.

The first time we met was when she came to pick me up at my home when it was time to go to Cali. She came through in a brand new Cadillac... Cocaine white.

It was a rental, but it was clean though. The drive was 26 hours with 2 gas stops, blowing weed the whole way. The homegirl ended up being super cool.

So when we got to LA, we of course hit up Roscoe's Chicken and Waffles and I remember having some country fried chicken with some white gravy and biscuits. At the time I was unsure about the gravy but I was feeling adventurous so I threw caution to the wind.

After we smashed our food, we got fresh and changed to meet up with Ira. I asked her if she could come along because it would be fun and by that point we got to know each other on the ride up. This was the first time I was going to meet him and we already had the "We in this thing together" type of feeling.

Nonetheless it was a huge party at a restaurant named Ago but it's pronounced Ah-go, so I was asked to meet him there. It happened to be on December 2, 2001. The VH1 My Music Awards After-Party.

When I tell you, I got the full Hollywood experience, that's putting it lightly. When we approached it was glitz, glam, lights, cameras and a line around the corner of all the people that wanted to get in, to catch a glimpse of their favorite star.

When we got there, I called to let him know we were outside. He appeared from the inside, walked towards the front and gestured with his hand, really more of a summoning, for us to come up. Letting us know we were good. We could pass the line and walk right in and we did exactly that.

One thing I've learned in life is when you're approaching a place you want to be, act as though you have been there before. Fuck fake it til you make it. You have to BE it before you SEE it. I felt great for "People" to be expecting me. I felt like I belonged.

So when we got in there, it definitely was a Who's Who of celebrities. He introduced me to everyone and they ALL knew him. I was mingling with them all, rubbing elbows and having drinks with some of the top players in Hollywood.

It seemed like Ira was the Go To Person because they ALL were in his face. I find it really funny and maybe even suspicious that I've been looking online for years trying to find him but he's incognito, hopefully he will resurface after this but I digress.

One of the first people I was introduced to was the VP of MTV. I can't remember his name but I remember he was well- dressed, average height about 5' 7", groomed short hair, and an older gentleman, at the time about 45-50 years old.

When I was introduced, it was like he had already talked to him about me. The reason I say this is because he leaned over in his ear and whispered something. I just acted country dumb like I didn't peep game.

After that, he led me to a circle conversation of females, then introduced me to Prince's female drummer at the time and Faith Evans. I even saw Ron Jeremy, I thought to myself this is the real deal and your girl ILL Skillz this is so amazing because I knew I wasn't tripping when people would look at me certain type of way when I would say my Store that's why I just shut up about it over the years but there's no way they shed me up, especially when the world is vindicating me of my story especially what's going on right now is in the building.

I was fanning out on the inside and couldn't believe that I was sitting here having a conversation with Faith Evans, and Prince's drummer like a regular day. This is the cooler talk I could get used to. I was sitting amidst music royalty, and I wanted to find my place among them.

I was laughing, dancing, and having a great time. Fine as hell, in my 20s, hustle on 100, and of course dressed to impress. I was high off of life. I had one, maybe 2 drinks so far because I wanted to keep a clear head, knowing that we were going to talk business at some point during the night. Mind you, I started drinking at like 13 years old so those drinks had none to minimal effect on me because my tolerance was high back then.

The homegirl Denia, pulls me to the side and reminds me of court in the morning so she had to burn out, but I was cool with it because I was there with Ira and we still had to talk business plus I didn't feel like there was any funny business going on.

So I thought.

I told her that it was fine for her to go, I would see her later and keep her phone on. It was nothing for me to be on a solo-dolo mission, especially when I'm focused on my end game and got my eye on the prize. So she ended up leaving and I stayed.

I was busy mingling and enjoying being in the moment of it all anyway. I'm in the middle of the club, dancing and vibing out. Then Ira asked me if I wanted another drink and he would go to the bar to get it for me.

I agreed but for a split second I thought about Rule #1 to A Girls Guide to Kickin It with Muthafuckas You Don't Know For Real- ALWAYS GET YOUR OWN DRINK AND KEEP YOUR EYES ON IT!! I did at least follow the second rule. ALWAYS MEET THEM AT A PUBLIC LOCATION, NEVER AT THE CRIB!!

But as far as the drink thing, the West Side in me knew better but I second guessed myself and thought, no problem because were going to be doing business together. That's how I looked at it so I didn't think anything of it.

At the time I was drinking Cranberry vodka and at that point that was my second or third drink. It was served in a medium-size glass tumbler with ice so they weren't strong. And plus I was feeling like, I'm in LA it's not like its a Saint Louis hole in the wall where they poured half of the bottle and your drink, with two ice cubes and a splash of juice for coloring. So at best I figured, here the drinks would be water down so I didn't have anything to worry about. So I thought.

So a little time goes by and I go to the bar to get some water. I remember being at the bar standing next to Jon Bon Jovi and Callista Lockhart and thinking Wow! She's the star of Ally McBeal! I watch that show every week. I'm even talking in my head like she be doing. This is GREAT!

I remember a waiter spilled some of a drink on Jon Bon Jovi, and I almost thought he was going to flip out because He's a cowboy, On a Steeeeel Horse He Rides! Hes Wanted (Waaaanteed) Dead or Alive!! but he was real chill about it and was more disappointed if anything, as we kind of looked and shook our heads about it, like "this guy".

He had a nice shirt on laughing it up with the pretty starlet, then all of a sudden in mid-giggle he gets sprayed like a wet t-shirt contest, with man-nips on display. I felt for him, it happens to the best of us. I got my water and left the crime scene and continued to mingle.

A few minutes later, everything started spinning and spinning and spinning and spinning like I was on a merry go round, but not quite that slow more like that other game that's at the playgrounds where everyone kind of jumps on with the metal handlebars and it goes round and around in a circle really fast and sometimes kids end up flying off and getting scuffed up. It felt more like that ride that you see on the playground in any hood park USA. Now put that ride in The House of Mirrors, where all of your spatial perception is distorted and dizzy.

My spirit said Exit stage left with the quickness, I did just that. As graceful and inconspicuous as my body would allow. In my head I was a gazelle, but in reality I probably was more like a sloth.

So I made my way to the ladies restroom, grabbed a wet paper towel and went into a stall to try to get myself together, sit down and gather my thoughts, because at the time I thought I was having a food poisoning episode from that Roscoe's Chicken and Waffles because like I said, I was suspicious of the white gravy and prior to that I had food poisoning at least twice before, within a year, so I was no stranger to it.

I thought that it attacked at the worst time ever and people may mistake me for the drunk girl at the party and that was my worst nightmare to be viewed as that and I knew I was far from it. Not saying I was never that but I retired that title by 21, albeit I will bust her out of retirement from time to time till this day but I was not here for that. I was here to do business and be amongst my future peers and I didnt want to ruin my reputation at my first Hollywood party.

I stayed in the bathroom for a long time. I remember getting sick and tossing my cookies. Then I told myself I'm just gonna close my eyes so I can get myself together. I didn't realize it but I passed out because by the time I woke up, rather I got awakened by a knock on my stall door by a woman's voice, saying Ira sent me in here to get you, we're getting ready to leave.

So I picked myself up off of the bathroom floor and pretended to be good, and did my best not to stumble out of the bathroom. When I walked back into the club, there were only a few stragglers left.

The club was a packed and busy, swanky place for celebrities when I went to the bathroom. I felt confused, like where did everybody go and how long was I in the bathroom but it was time to go, and the limousine was waiting so I left.

I'm thinking I have to pull myself together because we still haven't talked business.

I sat in the back of the limo, right between Ira and someone else to my left. We were on the way to the next destination. The After Party, of course! Normally I would have been all for it.

I mean, what aspiring entertainer looking to break into the business like a 2-11, wouldn't want to go to an exclusive Hollywood party, filled with present Stars, and future opportunities with the power to make sense of your past, by way of luxury transport. There's no reason to turn that down. So I thought.

The party must go on and on and on, till the break of dawn, seeing as though LA clubs close super early like 11pm. Everyone's laughing and drinking and I'm looking at them, feeling like things are moving in slo-mo. Champagne pouring, cocaine snorting. Models and bottles, going full throttle. You get the picture.

I'm sitting there trying to will the vomit away, which is threatening me like a Mama yelling from downstairs, at her kids roughhousing and tattling, Don't make me come UP there!! I'm begging like Please, Mama! No!! Especially when it seems like every bump in the road is being hit with precise measure, it was certain I was just prolonging the inevitable.

My head was still feeling like vertigo on crack. Either I was going to hurl in this limo, and all over the lovely ladies and luxurious things around me. Embarrass myself in front of all these good folks in front of me and ruin their night. Let's be honest, I don't care how much fun you are having, if someone throws up on you, it's time to go home, at least in my book. Or I could choose differently. I knew I had to make an executive decision.

I leaned over and whispered to Ira in true Hood Black Chick fashion, I made a simple request. "Can you raise the window down??". He said "Huh?" and I got a little louder in my tone. "Raise the window down, hit that window!".

As he proceeded to do so, simultaneously, I leaned over him and stuck my head out of the window to lose my lunch on the street instead of his lap. As the wind was blowing in my face, while I was leaving a trail of disgust in traffic, I happened to look at a street sign and thought to myself "So that's where Sunset and Vine is." Then continued to upchuck the rest of that country fried chicken from Roscoes.

I got my head back inside and sat down. I apologized and he said it was no big deal and that he has seen worse, but the rest of the passengers giggled and judged a bit but I was like whatever because I am aiming for a goal bigger than this limo ride. But at the same time I couldn't believe I was officially viewed as The Drunk Girl at the Party ". DAMN YOU, FOOD POISONING!!! So I thought.

We drove for a while and I asked Where are we going?. Ira said A party in The Hills . I was unfamiliar but I was there to ride it out because we still haven't discussed any type of business, we've just been kickin it. So after a bunch of twists and turns we arrive at the destination.

As I scoot out of the back seat and raise my head for things to come into view, I rise to see a magnificent dwelling. Prestigious in statute with lights shining all over it. It was a palace in my eyes.

I grew up on the west side of St. Louis in a 2 family flat. Although my father was an African Chief, me and my siblings never lived the lifestyle since we were abandoned but I've heard stories of the royal shit that went on.

Looking at that multi-million dollar mansion, I thought to myself I am FINALLY living my REAL life!. The life that I somehow missed out on from being left in America with my mother, brother and sister, while the other part of my 6 siblings lived in misery in Nigeria with Dear Ol' Dad.

I took a deep breath and got out with the rest of the group. We piled out in succession. In spite of battling my physical difficulties that I was dealing with, I managed to take it all in. I looked down the long, swiveling driveway and it all was secluded with native foliage draping around the perimeter. There were tall, white Roman-Greco columns standing like guards in front of Fort Knox. I proceeded up the steps and through the oversized, grand doorway and entered the foyer.

It was as big as some people's entire homes. There was a huge, curved staircase that wrapped around to the top floor. There was artwork and decor furnishing the ambiance, colored with pearl and gold.

The rest of the group sniggled and giggled their way into the main room and I almost followed behind them but the head spinning picked up where it left off and my stomach told me I had a meeting in the ladies room. I asked the first person that looked at me Where is your bathroom?. They pointed to my left and said It's right there. I immediately walked in that direction and closed the door behind me and locked it.

This was not your average dumpsite. No, no, no, my dear. It was enormous and deluxe with a porcelain throne fit for a king. If I could just make it there. I stood at the door for a moment to visually calculate the distance. I could feel the sickness approaching at a rapid rate because behind closed doors all of my defenses were down and I didnt need to fake the funk since no one was looking.

The room really got to spinning. It was like I heard the sound effects of the dizziness. It reminded me of the sound Kit made on Knight Rider. Woo-Woom Woo-Woom. I was declining fast. I wobbled my way to the toilet, kicking my shoes off on the way there.

I collapsed on the floor close enough to throw up whenever it came. I laid there, with my cheek laying against the coldness. I thought to myself. "Man, this floor feels sooooooo goood. Wait, is this Marble?? This is some nice shit! These people got some money, money!"

I couldn't believe I was in the bathroom attempting to get it together for the umpteenth time. Dipping off like I can't hold my liquor and I only had two or a few drinks. This is some bullshit.

What kind of impression am I making? Obviously not a good one. I'm in the middle of my dream and I can't be awake enough to enjoy it, I thought to myself. I'm just gonna close my eyes for a few minutes and go out there and be the life of the party. Next thing I knew I heard a knock on the door and a voice saying on the other end Ira is ready to go I was like Whaaaat??, Damn!, How long I was here? It happened again. I fucked around and missed the whole thing.

I was disoriented. You know the kind of disorientation that you get when you get snatched out of your sleep and someone starts asking you calculus level questions. I opened the door and I looked back towards the main room before I walked out of the front door.

I wondered what I missed and what "went down" in there. I was just glad my head started to clear up a bit but it by far wasn't where it needed to be. We got in a vehicle but I'm not sure it was the limo but we got from point A to B.

I followed the flow because although we have spent a substantial amount of time together we still haven't talked about the point of it all. The business part. My career. Us making some big bucks and rolling in the dough. That was the conversation I was looking to have but I knew it was coming because all of this couldn't possibly be in vain. So onward we go.

The destination of point B was his best friend's house. I said Okay cool, I'm game. We drove for a while and pull up to Bestie's house, really a condo, and when we walked in he introduced me. I was so surprised and couldn't even believe who he was and an unlikely pair of friends I thought to myself.

It was Darius McCrary- Eddie Fucking Winslow from Family Matters. I grew up watching him and Erkel and shit. "I am well on my way " I thought to myself.

Ira and him joked and chit chatted for a minute while Eddie's house guest talked about how much she wanted to go shopping with his credit card- some slim model chick with long brown hair-Caucasian Persuasion. Then Ira took me to the spare bedroom, got some extra blankets and said he hoped I felt better.

I apologized for the night and told him I think it was some food that I ate earlier. He was understanding and said he would see me in the morning and we could talk about why I came. That was relieving because I thought I'd royally screwed things up. Him saying that calmed my nerves enough to put my mind at ease.

I laid there waiting for tomorrow to come. Waiting for my life to change. Although Ira seemed cool but I'm still in unfamiliar surroundings and far away from home. I grew up on the West Side so I will always have my guards up, ready for things to go left. I locked the door, slept with my clothes on and my pants buttoned. The room was still spinning but not as fast.

Ira said he had a son with Chaka Khan. I don't know how valid that part is but he was very well connected in the industry so I went along with it. If they don't have a son together, then this man lied on her pussy like a mug.

Nowadays that information can be found out but back then you just kinda had to take their word for it until proven otherwise. Made up and straight fabricated a whole human being if it's not the truth but most of Hollywood or hollow- wood because it's so shallow and full of smoke and mirrors and make-believe.

The Morning After the Mirage

This deal, he's been dangling it like a carrot on a string. Because up until that point, all we had done was go on a whirlwind wild goose chase. I drifted off to sleep thinking, Tomorrow is the day.

It's go-time. Morning comes. Ira pops into the room, all chipper-like, checking on me. He's like, Rough night, huh? I'm like, Yeah, it was... pretty rough, trying to laugh it off. I thanked him for taking care of me because, truth be told, in my mind I was still thinking I had caught an epic case of food poisoning. I mean, that gravy at Roscoes was suspect.

And here's the kicker:

At that point, I actually thought, Wow... he's a good guy. He didn't even try to take advantage of me while I was over here looking like a hot mess. Maybe he's really decent.

Cue the clown music.

We're sitting on the bed, and then Ira leans in all serious-like and says, "I can take your career exactly where you want it to go..."

And I'm thinking, Yes! Finally! This is it!

I sat up straighter, excitement bubbling under the surface, ready to talk about studio sessions, tours, contracts and all the good shit.

Then this fool hits me with:

"But what are you gonna do for me?"

I sat there blinking like a confused baby deer.

"What do you mean, what am I gonna do for you?"

I started rambling, flustered as hell:

"I'm gonna work really hard! I'm gonna make great music! We're gonna make a lot of money together! I'm gonna blow up and make you proud!"

But deep down... my stomach dropped.

I knew exactly what he meant.

That unspoken quid pro quo hung heavy between us.

This was the BIG reveal. This was the price nobody talks about when they say they made it.

We were at a stalemate.

He looked at me. I looked at him.

And in that moment, we both knew.

He knew I wasn't giving IT up. And I knew he wasn't going to hand over that golden ticket without IT.

Looking back now, I know God was all up in through that situation. He protected me from all of it.

Because Ira didn't have anything on me, no compromising photos, no dirt, no forced hand. No contract signed in drunken desperation. Nothing.

And trust me, if he had it, he would have used it. That's the way Hollywood moves.

So yes, I was disappointed. Heartbroken isn't even the right word, it was more like disenchanted.

The dream I came chasing was right there at the doorstep...

But I wasn't willing to pay the dirty-ass cover charge.

I realized that night: The mystery of the Hollywood dream... is that it ain't really a dream at all.

It's an exposure to who you are, who they are, and what you're really willing to trade to sit at their table.

And baby, I chose me!

Volume I – Chapter 6: Soul Contracts, Divine Playpens & Healing the Inner Child

---

Volume I – Chapter 6: Soul Contracts, Divine Playpens & Healing the Inner Child

Section 1: The Divine Playpen Principle

Subtitle: Earth Ain't a Prison—It's a Classroom with Padding

"God didn't send you here to be punished. God sent you here to play, fall, cry, and climb again—until you remembered who you were all along."

One day, while sitting with my thoughts and trying to make peace with all the painful shit I'd survived—broken relationships, family wounds, near-death crashes, childhood confusion, betrayal—I had an epiphany drop in my spirit like a soft lightning bolt:

"Earth is a divine playpen."

Not a prison. Not a mistake. But a safe-enough zone where souls come to test ideas, try on identities, and make divine messes while learning how to come back to wholeness. A playpen has soft sides for a reason—

it's made to catch the falls. So is this place. So is this life.

We aren't here because we're being punished. We're here because God trusted us enough to play.

To explore.

To feel it all.

To figure it out.

To remember.

Your inner child wasn't broken. She was overwhelmed in a world that forgot it was a playpen. But God never forgot. And neither did your soul. You came here to evolve—yes—but also to experience wonder. To learn how to create again with your imagination turned all the way on.

Scientific Insight: The Power of Play on Brain Development

Neuroscientists have proven that play is essential to healthy brain development in children. It improves memory, creativity, emotional regulation, and social intelligence. What many don't realize is that the adult brain still responds to play in powerful ways— releasing dopamine, forming new neural pathways, and dissolving stress hormones.

When we stop playing, we don't just become adults—we become spiritually brittle.

But when we return to play, even for a moment, we open the neural gate to joy, curiosity, and healing. And that's not just therapy. That's reactivation of divine memory.

Universal Law: The Law of Polarity

In a divine playpen, you need contrast to learn. You need up and down. Yes and no. Love and loss. The Law of Polarity teaches that everything contains its opposite—and through experiencing one, you gain access to understanding the other. Earth, in all its chaos and contradiction, is where you learn how to choose alignment by seeing what it feels like to be out of it.

Personal Experience

I used to ask God, "Why would you let that happen to me?" especially during some of my most painful chapters. And I didn't get a booming voice or lightning flash. I got a memory—of myself as a child, creating imaginary worlds in a closet, believing magic was real, knowing I was never alone.

That was the divine playpen. And it was always there. Even in the darkest moments, there was an unseen safety net catching me—not stopping every fall, but cushioning the impact so I could learn, grow, and still get back up.

When I looked at my life through that lens, I didn't feel cursed anymore. I felt chosen.

Not for pain—but for expansion.

Ritual: Re-enter the Playpen

Do this ritual when life feels too heavy and your inner child is begging to breathe.

What You'll Need:

- A childhood toy or item (or something playful like bubbles, crayons, or a favorite snack)

- A space where you won't be judged for being silly

- A willingness to let go

Steps:

1. Hold the item or place it nearby. Close your eyes and say:

   "I give my inner child permission to come

out and play."

2. Put on a playful song, or just sit and daydream.

3. Let yourself giggle, hum, color, dance, snack—without justification.

4. After 5–10 minutes, speak aloud:

   "Earth is my playpen. God is not mad at me. I am here to learn, not to suffer."

5. Finish by thanking your inner child for showing up.

You just reset the energy field.

Journal Reflection:

What parts of your life have felt like punishment—and how might seeing them as part of a soul classroom shift your perspective?

Affirmation:

"I am not here to be punished. I am here to play, learn, and remember. Earth is my sacred sandbox and I trust the divine design."

Volume I – Chapter 6: Soul Contracts, Divine Playpens & Healing the Inner Child

Section 2: Earth Is a Laboratory Too

Subtitle: Divine Experiments & Explosions

"Sometimes the mess was the method. You weren't failing—you were running field tests for your next level."

While Earth is a playground for spiritual learning, it's also a laboratory for divine experimentation. You didn't come here to be perfect. You came here to test reality. To mix belief systems, combine experiences, and see what reactions occur.

In this sacred lab, your thoughts are hypotheses.

Your choices? The variables.

Your results? Data.

Sometimes you blow up a friendship.

Sometimes a relationship goes up in flames.

Sometimes you go bankrupt, relapse, walk away, or melt down.

And guess what? It's all part of the lab work.

You're here learning the laws of energy, alchemy, karma, and creation through real-world experimentation. Even when you feel like you "messed it up," you actually collected the evidence you needed to grow wiser, braver, and more aligned.

No divine scientist is punished for mixing the wrong formula—because the lesson is in the reaction. The Divine Playpen was your reminder that you are held.

The Divine Lab is your permission to try again. Explode again. Innovate again.

You are the sacred chemist of your life, and Earth is your multidimensional classroom, your sandbox, and your lab.

Ritual: The Alchemist's Reframe

Take a moment to write down a moment in life where something "blew up." A loss, failure, heartbreak, or embarrassment.

Now reframe it like a scientific discovery:

- What were you testing?

- What ingredients went in?

- What did the reaction reveal?

- What did you learn?

Burn or release the paper in water as a sacred symbol of transmutation. Say aloud:

"That wasn't a mistake. That was an experiment. And I learned the formula."

Scientific Insight:

Neuroscience shows that trial-and-error learning strengthens neural pathways and builds emotional resilience. Just as muscles grow by being torn and rebuilt, so does our emotional and energetic intelligence through repeated testing and re-alignment.

Universal Law – The Law of Correspondence:

As within, so without. As above, so below.

Your internal experiments reflect outward experiences. The universe mirrors your energetic trials and brings external results to match your internal formula. Change the ingredients, and the outcome shifts.

Journal Prompt:

"What patterns, emotions, or experiences keep showing up in my life as opportunities to test, tweak, or transform? If I treated my life as a spiritual laboratory—where failure is feedback and experiments lead to wisdom—what would I give myself permission to try, break, rebuild, or redefine?"

Affirmation:

"I am a divine experimenter. Every explosion was part of my evolution. I extract wisdom from the wreckage and I alchemize the lesson into light."

Volume I – Chapter 6: Soul Contracts, Divine Playpens & Healing the Inner Child

Section 3: Shadow Work & Emotional Triggers

Subtitle: When Pain Points Become Portals to Power

"The things that trigger you aren't trying to destroy you—they're trying to deliver you."

Let's be real: sometimes healing don't feel holy. Sometimes it feels like rage, tears, or shutting down when someone says something that hits a nerve you didn't know was exposed. That's the shadow calling. That's the inner child knocking.

Triggers aren't the problem. They're the notification.

Every time you get defensive, feel rejected, or overreact to something "small," your body is telling you there's an old wound still running the show. It's not weakness—it's programming. And until we stop seeing our triggers as enemies, we'll keep missing the divine messages hiding inside them.

One day I got so mad over something tiny—like not being listened to—that I had to pause and ask, "Why does this keep happening? Why does this hurt so bad?"

And boom. The answer was in a memory I hadn't consciously thought about in years: a childhood moment where I was overlooked, unheard, and felt invisible. That pain didn't die—it went underground. And it kept popping up through adult experiences, trying to get my attention.

That's what shadow work is.

Not fighting the dark, but sitting in it long enough to find your younger self waiting to be understood.

Scientific Insight: Trauma and the Nervous System

When you experience trauma or emotional wounding, your brain encodes it—especially if it happened repeatedly or early in life. These experiences become implicit memories, stored in the body. Later in life, similar situations can trigger those stored patterns— even if they're not logically connected.

This is why you might feel rage when someone interrupts you, or shame when someone disagrees with you—it's your nervous system replaying old emotional footage.

Shadow work helps you bring conscious awareness to unconscious programming, rewire your reactions, and reclaim your peace.

Universal Law: The Law of Cause and Effect

Nothing shows up in your emotional world without a root. Every reaction has a cause—even if it's buried. The Law of Cause and Effect reminds us that what seems like a surface issue is often the echo of a deeper origin. Shadow work lets us trace the echo back to its source—and change the vibration at the root.

Personal Experience

I remember one argument where I felt totally dismissed. And not just frustrated—wounded. Like I wanted to scream, "I matter too!" And it hit me: that wasn't about this moment. That was the little girl in me—trying to be heard by people who were too broken to listen.

I used to think being triggered meant I was unstable. Now I know it means I'm healing.

The wounds that were buried are surfacing so I can finally give them air, love, and closure.

Ritual: Meet the Trigger, Meet the Child

Do this ritual when you feel reactive or overwhelmed by an emotional trigger.

What You'll Need:

- A quiet space

- A pen and notebook

- A willingness to get real with yourself

Steps:

1. When a trigger hits, pause. Breathe. Ask:

   "What age am I feeling right now?"

2. Close your eyes and let your body answer. Picture that version of yourself.

3. In your notebook, write a letter from that younger self, even just a sentence. Let them speak.

4. Respond as your current self with love, validation, and safety.

5. Say aloud:

   "Thank you for showing me what still needed my love. You are safe now."

This ritual turns emotional explosions into healing conversations.

Journal Reflection:

What recurring emotional triggers do you experience—and what younger version of you might be trying to speak through them?

Affirmation:

"My triggers are teachers. I no longer silence my shadow—I sit with it, heal with it, and rise from it."

Volume I – Chapter 6: Soul Contracts, Divine Playpens & Healing the Inner Child
Section 4: Healing the Inner Child for Manifestation Mastery

Subtitle: Reparenting Yourself Back to Wholeness and Receiving

"You can't fully receive until the child in you feels safe to believe."

You can journal, vision board, and speak affirmations all day, but if the child in you is still holding onto fear, shame, or unworthiness... your manifestations will keep short-circuiting.

Why?

Because your inner child is the gatekeeper to your subconscious mind—and that's where real manifestation happens.

If you grew up being told you were too much, not enough, ignored, silenced, abused, or made to feel invisible... the part of you that was meant to believe in magic got injured. And without healing that part, your adult self may want love, success, and abundance—but the child in you doesn't feel safe to receive it.

I had to learn this the hard way. I was doing all the manifesting techniques, but something still felt blocked. That's when it hit me: I needed to go back for the girl who was waiting to be picked up.

Not by someone else—but by me.

I didn't need another mentor or lover or guru.

I needed to reparent myself.

I needed to say to her, "I see you. I'm sorry you had to go through that. And I've got you now."

And you know what happened?

Shifts. Real shifts.

Opportunities flowed. My voice got louder. My manifestations landed faster.

Because the child in me finally trusted that the adult me was safe enough to let them dream again.

Scientific Insight: Inner Child Healing & Subconscious Rewiring

The subconscious mind—where most manifestation occurs—is formed primarily between the ages of 0–7. During this time, children absorb beliefs through emotional experiences, not logic.

When you revisit and reprogram those early beliefs, you literally change the frequency of what you're aligned with.

Psychology confirms that inner child work helps regulate the nervous system, decrease anxiety, and increase self-worth—all of which open the body and mind to receiving more love, wealth, and creative flow.

Universal Law: The Law of Mentalism

"All is mind."

Your thoughts, beliefs, and inner dialogues shape your reality. If the child in you still believes they're not worthy, the universe mirrors that belief. But when you heal and upgrade that mental blueprint, you become magnetic—because your inner world aligns with what you say you want.

Personal Experience

There were moments I was praised publicly but still felt empty inside. And I realized: praise doesn't land when the child in you still feels unseen.

So I stopped waiting for the world to validate me and became my own safe space.

I bought myself little gifts. I sang to myself in the mirror. I let my inner child play with hairstyles, color, dance, and joy.

Every time I honored her, my life got lighter.

And the magic came faster.

Ritual: Meet Your Inner Child at the Gate

Do this ritual when you feel blocked, stuck, or afraid to dream big.

What You'll Need:

- A childhood photo of yourself

- A pen and notebook

- A small item to represent comfort (blanket, plush toy, etc.)

Steps:

1. Look at the photo. Really look. Say: "You are safe with me now."

2. In your journal, let the child in you speak. What do they need? What are they afraid of?

3. Write a letter to them as your adult self. Comfort them. Invite them into your vision.

4. Hold or place the comfort item over your heart. Close your eyes and visualize your inner child stepping into your current life—free, smiling, and ready to co-create with you.

Journal Reflection:

What would your inner child create, become, or receive if they truly felt safe, seen, and supported?

Affirmation:

"My inner child is healed, heard, and home. Together, we create a life of magic, joy, and divine overflow."

Volume I – Chapter 7: Reprogramming Your Man-chine and Your Mental Garden

---

Volume I – Chapter 7: Reprogramming Your Man-chine and Your Mental Garden

Section 1: Mental Food- You Are What You Think

Subtitle: Mastering the Mind, Tending the Thoughts, and Coding the Field

"You are not broken. You're programmable. And baby, it's time to write new software for your soul."

You are more than flesh and feeling—you are a bio-spiritual computer, a divine "man-chine" designed to receive, transmit, and create reality through your thoughts, emotions, and frequency field. The problem is, most people are running outdated programming.

Trauma-coded thoughts.

Inherited belief systems.

Low-vibration loops downloaded in childhood and reinforced by culture, family, and media.

But just like a phone or a laptop, you can delete what's no longer serving, install new systems, and upgrade your inner operating code. In this chapter, we'll explore how to reprogram your man-chine, rewire your inner dialogue, and replant your mental garden so you're not just surviving—you're creating intentionally.

You'll learn how to identify corrupted thought files, clear the cache of past pain, speak life into your field, and become the conscious coder of your reality. You'll understand why solitude is a sacred reset, why words are spell-craft, and how to align your internal system with the frequency of abundance, peace, and purpose.

It's not about perfection.

It's about power.

And remembering—you hold the pen, the keyboard, and the code.

Volume I – Chapter 7: Reprogramming Your Man-chine and Your Mental Garden

Section 2: Understanding the Man-chine (Human Divine Technology)

Subtitle: You Are Not Just Using Technology—You Are Technology

"The brain is the hardware, the mind is the software, and the soul is the power source. You are the device and the divine plug."

We've been taught to treat technology like it's something separate from us—out there, on screens, in devices. But the deeper truth? You are divine technology. A spiritual instrument wrapped in biological code. A walking transmitter, receiver, processor, and power plant.

I call it the man-chine—part man, part machine, fully God-powered.

You're a chemical reactor. A biological conductor. An emotional hard drive storing programs from childhood, culture, trauma, joy, and everything in between. Every thought is a signal. Every emotion is a code. Every vibration is a command you're broadcasting into the quantum field—and it responds like a perfectly synced algorithm.

We update our phones more often than we update our minds. But the mind is the mainframe. And most of us are still running on the spiritual equivalent of Windows '95.

It's not your fault if you were programmed in dysfunction.

But it is your power to reprogram with intention.

Scientific Insight: Your Body Is Bioelectric

The human body runs on electricity—literally. Your brain sends signals using electrical impulses. Your heart creates an electromagnetic field 60 times greater than your brain. Nerve cells communicate through synapses, generating voltage. This isn't poetic—it's physics.

And just like a machine, if the wiring is frayed or overloaded by stress, trauma, or toxic thoughts, the system crashes—in the form of burnout, illness, anxiety, depression, or chronic disconnection.

But here's the power move: You can reboot the system. You can rewrite the code.

Universal Law: The Law of Mentalism

"All is mind. The universe is mental."

This Hermetic principle teaches that everything begins as a thought. Your reality is not just shaped by your mind—it is a projection of it. If you want to change your outer world, you must first update your internal program.

Your man-chine responds to commands. Speak accordingly.

Personal Experience

When I started treating my mind like a sacred motherboard, everything changed. I stopped feeding it junk thoughts. I deleted guilt files. I rewrote scripts that were planted in me by other people's fears. I started talking to my cells, blessing my body, and running diagnostics on my moods.

After my accident, when my memory was foggy and my energy was low, I realized how powerful my internal system really was. Healing wasn't just physical—it was mental firmware recovery. I had to manually reinstall joy, trust, and vision every single day until my system caught up with the command.

Ritual: Divine System Scan

Do this when you feel off, unfocused, or mentally cluttered.

What You'll Need:

- A quiet space

- A notebook or recording app

- A mirror (optional)

Steps:

1. Sit still and say aloud:

> "System scan initiated. I am checking my energetic software."

2. Ask: "What thoughts are looping in me that no longer serve?"

3. Write or speak the first 3-5 answers that come up.

4. Now say:

> "Delete. Clear cache. Reinstall divine truth."

5. Replace each thought with a powerful affirmation or vision (e.g., "I am capable. I am expanding. I am safe.")

Optional: Look in the mirror and say, "System online. God frequency restored."

Journal Reflection:

What old belief or mental program are you ready to uninstall—and what new code will you replace it with?

Affirmation:

"I am a divine man-chine. My mind is sacred code. My soul is the Source. I align, update, and radiate divine intelligence."

Volume I – Chapter 7: Reprogramming Your Man-chine and Your Mental Garden
Section 3: Solitude as a Sacred Reset

Subtitle: Alone Doesn't Mean Abandoned

"The quiet isn't empty. It's pregnant with answers. Solitude is where God speaks the loudest."

At one point in my life, I confused being alone with being unloved. I mistook stillness for stagnation. I thought that if nobody was calling, visiting, or checking on me, I must have done something wrong. But baby, let me tell you—some of the deepest upgrades happen in isolation.

Solitude is not punishment. It's programming time. It's when God pulls you aside to reboot your frequency, clean out distractions, and install divine downloads you couldn't receive with all the background noise.

Some of your best transformations will not be witnessed.

Some of your greatest breakthroughs will look like breakdowns to others.

But when the divine wants to speak clearly, it turns down the volume on everything else.

Solitude doesn't mean you're losing—it means you're leveling up in private.

Scientific Insight: Solitude and Brain Clarity

Neuroscience has shown that solitude enhances clarity, memory consolidation, creativity, and self-awareness. It resets your default mode network—a brain system that activates when the mind is at rest—and allows your thoughts to organize themselves.

Extended solitude helps regulate cortisol (stress hormone), balances the nervous system, and restores energetic boundaries. This isn't just a "vibe"—it's biological and neurological renewal.

Universal Law: The Law of Rhythm

Everything moves in cycles—action and rest, expansion and contraction, social and solitary. The Law of Rhythm reminds us that solitude is a natural phase of becoming. You're not "missing out"—you're being refined in rhythm with divine timing.

Personal Experience

There were times when I felt completely forgotten by people I once held down. I'd be the one showing up, giving rides, feeding folks, encouraging dreams—but when my soul needed support, the room got quiet. That silence used to sting. But then I realized:

God was getting everyone out the way.

So I could hear ME.

So I could hear GOD.

Some of my deepest revelations—about who I am, what I carry, and what I came here to do—came in the silence after the noise. In the stillness after the heartbreak. In the moments when I had to look in the mirror and say, "I got you."

Solitude taught me I wasn't abandoned—I was being anointed.

Ritual: Sacred Reset in Solitude

Use this ritual when you feel emotionally cluttered, socially drained, or uncertain about your next move.

What You'll Need:

- A quiet space

- A candle or dim light

- A blanket or comfortable seat

Steps:

1. Turn off all devices. Let the silence be the sacred space.

2. Sit in stillness for 7 minutes (set a gentle timer).

   Don't try to meditate—just be.

3. As thoughts come up, observe them like clouds. Don't chase them.

4. Whisper this aloud:

   "I am safe in this silence. My soul is resetting. My path is revealing."

5. Wrap yourself in the blanket or place your hand on your chest and say:

   "Even alone, I am never abandoned. Even silent, I am deeply heard."

Let that be enough. Let the quiet hold you.

Journal Reflection:

What has solitude taught you that you couldn't learn in the noise of others?

Affirmation:

"Solitude is my sacred sanctuary. In stillness, I reset. In silence, I hear divine truth."

Volume I – Chapter 7: Reprogramming Your Man-chine and Your Mental Garden

Section 4: The Karmic Credit Card

Subtitle: Paying Your Spiritual Debt

"You can also accumulate spiritual debt... and there are no payment arrangements."

Just like you can rack up financial debt from overspending, you can also accumulate karmic debt from the energy you put into the world.

Every intention, every lie, every betrayal, every selfish action—those don't just disappear.

They create a vibrational deficit. A negative imprint in your soul account.

And no matter how much you want to manifest blessings, you can't swipe your way into alignment when your spiritual balance is in the red.

This is karmic law.

And in the Court of Karma, everything is ruled with divine fairness and energetic receipts.

You might escape human judgment.

You might even fool the public.

But you can't finesse the field.

Because the field is energy. It keeps score through vibration.

The Karmic Credit Card – A Metaphysical Metaphor

Think of every wrongdoing or violation against your own soul or others as a spiritual swipe.

At first, it might seem like there are no consequences—like you got away with it.

But baby, the bill always comes due.

The karmic credit card allows you to run up a balance, but you must pay it off—whether in this lifetime or the next.

And the gag is:

You choose your own repayment plan through your experiences.

You pay through:

- Accountability

- Apologies

- Altruism

- Inner work

- Making it right with those you harmed

- Or living through what you put others through

Why You Can't Manifest Fully with Unpaid Karma

Manifestation isn't just mindset—it's magnetic alignment.

If your field is carrying energetic debt, it will block the full flow of your blessings.

Not as punishment, but as protection and balance.

God doesn't bless mess.

Not because God is petty—but because the law of energetic harmony must be restored first.

You can't build a mansion on top of unpaid karma.

You must level the energetic land before you pour your spiritual foundation.

How to Pay Off Karmic Debt:

1. Take spiritual inventory – Be honest about the pain you've caused or avoided.

2. Ask for divine clarity – "Show me what I must make right."

3. Do the opposite – Overcorrect the pattern. Be what you weren't.

4. Make offerings – Not just to the Divine, but to those you harmed.

5. Clean your field with integrity – Not just crystals and sage—but character and accountability.

Scientific Insight: Epigenetics & Energetic Patterning

Studies in epigenetics show that trauma, behavior, and even shame can be passed through DNA.

What we don't repair, we repeat.

What we don't face, our children may feel.

Karmic debt isn't just spiritual—it's biological memory, stored in your very code.

Universal Law – The Law of Cause and Effect

Also known as the Law of Karma: Every cause creates an effect.

Every action has a reaction.

Your karmic credit score is determined by what you create, ignore, and repair.

Journal Prompt:

"What cycle in my life feels like a bill that keeps coming back? How can I make a soul payment on that debt through truth, action, or healing?"

Affirmation:

"I release all patterns that keep me indebted to past versions of myself. I honor divine justice. I restore balance with action, truth, and sacred repair."

Volume I – Chapter 7: Reprogramming Your Man-chine and Your Mental Garden

Section 5: Power of Words – Speaking Life Into Your Field

Subtitle: Spells, Scripts, and the Vibration of Your Voice

"You're not just talking—you're coding. Every word is a wand."

Words aren't just sound. They are frequencies. They are formulas. And whether you realize it or not, you've been casting spells your whole life.

Every "I can't" has written a line of code.

Every "I am" has summoned something into your field.

Every idle joke, passive dig, or harsh self-talk has left an energetic imprint.

That's why the ancients called it "spelling." Because every word is a spell.

And you? You're the magician—either cursing or blessing yourself with your mouth.

I had to catch myself one day. I kept saying things like, "I'm tired," "I can't win," "Nothing ever goes right."

And guess what? My body got more tired. My field got heavier. My mood got funkier. That wasn't life attacking me—that was my vibration creating a script and the Universe responding to it like an obedient echo.

Once I realized this, I started speaking differently.

Not because I was in denial—but because I was in creation mode.

Scientific Insight: Sound Frequencies & Brain Chemistry

Sound—especially the spoken word—creates neural and chemical shifts. When you speak positively, your brain releases feel-good neurotransmitters like dopamine and serotonin. Affirmations and vocal tones have also been shown to reduce cortisol and increase focus.

And since your vocal cords vibrate through your entire body, you are literally tuning your field every time you speak. It's like striking a tuning fork inside your chest.

Universal Law: The Law of Vibration

Everything is in motion. Every word you speak has a vibrational signature, and it attracts according to its frequency. Speak in fear, and you'll match with experiences that confirm it. Speak in faith, and life will rise to meet your sound.

Words don't just describe your world—they build it.

Personal Experience

There was a time when my words were loose—sarcastic, doubtful, even self-sabotaging. I'd say things like "I'll never catch a break" or "I'm always broke" and laugh it off. But the Universe doesn't understand jokes—it understands vibration.

Once I caught that revelation, I tightened my tongue.

I became surgical with my words.

I stopped agreeing with struggle and started declaring overflow.

And slowly but surely, my field shifted.

Even now, when I feel down, I speak life until I feel truth catch up.

Because if I don't speak for me, who will?

Ritual: Speak Life Into Your Field

Use this ritual when you're in a low state, doubting yourself, or needing to re-code your energy.

What You'll Need:

- A mirror (or voice recorder)

- A quiet space

- A written list of "I AM" statements (create your own or use examples)

Steps:

1. Stand in front of the mirror or open your voice recorder.

2. Read your "I AM" list aloud—slowly, clearly, like sacred commands.

3. After each statement, pause and feel it in your chest.

4. Say this closing invocation:

   "My words are sacred. My voice is my vibration. My sound creates my reality."

Repeat daily until you believe it—and then keep going.

Journal Reflection:

What recurring words or phrases do you say about yourself—and are they casting curses or building blessings?

Affirmation:

"My voice is divine. My words are sacred. I speak with power, purpose, and precision—coding my field with truth."

Volume I – Chapter 8: From Wishing to Manifesting – Quick Guide Companion

---

Volume I – Chapter 8: From Wishing to Manifesting – Quick Guide Companion

Section 1: Music as Code

Subtitle: The Sonic Spellbook

"Some songs weren't just catchy—they were coded. Every chorus a chant. Every beat a broadcast. Music is the language of the gods disguised as entertainment."

Music isn't just background noise—it's a vibrational spell.

From lullabies to love songs, from battle hymns to ballads—music has always been a way to code emotion, store memory, and transmit messages across time.

But beneath the surface of chart-toppers and nursery rhymes lies something deeper:

A sonic spellbook.

An energetic archive of spells, affirmations, and subconscious commands that either liberate or lull the mind.

Some songs are rituals in disguise.

Others are soul contracts sung aloud.

And many are used by those in power to manipulate collective vibration—because music doesn't just influence mood, it programs reality.

Sound Is the First Code

In the beginning was the word—but before the word, there was frequency.

The cosmic "OM", the vibrational hum of creation, the soundless sound that rippled across the void and formed galaxies.

Every frequency carries a message. Every beat carves structure into matter.

Experiments in cymatics prove this: sound vibrations placed beneath sand, water, or plasma form sacred geometry, depending on the frequency.

That means music is more than emotional—it's structural.

Songs don't just affect how we feel—they shape how we form.

Lyrics as Locked Codes

What if the lyrics we recite are actually spells we cast?

Think about this:

- "Row, row, row your boat…"

    - Teaches co-creation and the illusion of control in a dream-like realm.

- "Hotel California" by the Eagles

    - A metaphorical trap of spiritual stagnation and elite occult systems.

- "No Church in the Wild" by Jay Z & Kanye

    - A philosophical rebellion against organized programming and a question of what morality truly means.

Many lyrics hide esoteric teachings, elite messaging, or divine downloads wrapped in rhythm.

These aren't accidents—they're energetic installations.

Subconscious Programming Through Sound

Neurologically, music bypasses the analytical mind.

It enters the limbic system (emotion), the amygdala (fear/pleasure), and even the hippocampus (memory).

That's why you can recall every lyric to a song from 20 years ago—but forget where your keys are.

The repetition of lyrics combined with emotional resonance = spellwork.

You are literally singing incantations into your subconscious. Over and over again.

This is how collective beliefs are shaped.

This is how we've been programmed—and how we can reprogram ourselves.

Divine Artists and Sonic Alchemists

Some artists act as vessels.

Their music carries activation codes, healing frequencies, or warnings hidden in plain sight.

Examples from your vision:

- Travis Scott's "Antidote" is more than a drug metaphor—it's a call to awaken to poison vs. cure in an artificial reality.

- Lauryn Hill's entire discography is a spiritual curriculum in disguise.

- Even pop or hip-hop can carry binary messages:

Those who know, hear the deeper layers.
Those who don't, just dance.

This is why ancient cultures treated music as sacred technology—not entertainment.

The drum was a portal. The chant was a map. The melody was medicine.

Ritual: Your Personal Sonic Spellbook

1. Make a playlist of songs that uplift, activate, and align you.

2. Reflect on lyrics that you've unknowingly sung for years—are they spells you no longer consent to?

3. Create a "mantra track" using your own affirmations, beats, or chanting. Listen daily.

Let your ears become your altar.

Scientific Insight: Water, Sound & Memory

Your body is over 70% water.

Water holds vibrational memory—proven in the studies of Dr. Masaru Emoto, who showed that water molecules change shape when exposed to love, hate, music, and prayer.

When you listen to music, you are reprogramming the molecular memory of your body.

You're either hydrating your field with harmony or dissonance. Choose wisely.

Universal Law: The Law of Vibration

Everything moves. Everything vibrates.

This law governs all sound, emotion, and manifestation.

To change your reality, you must change your frequency.

And music is one of the fastest ways to do that.

Scientific Insight: Phonetics, Symbolism & Subconscious Programming

The subconscious mind doesn't speak English—it speaks symbol, repetition, tone, and imagery. That's why emojis are so powerful. That's why phonetic words carry weight—because sound and symbol cut deeper than sentence structure.

Studies in neurolinguistics have shown that the emotional tone of language affects the brain more than the logic of the words themselves. Meaning: your mood and intent matter more than the dictionary definition.

Journal Prompt:

"If my soul had a soundtrack, what songs would be on it—and what spells have they cast over my identity, my healing, or my beliefs?"

Affirmation:

"I decode the lyrics of my life. I choose sound that heals, activates, and elevates my vibration. I am the DJ of my destiny."

Volume I – Chapter 8: From Wishing to Manifesting – Quick Guide Companion

Section 2: Power of Play – Using Joy to Unlock Energy Flow

Subtitle: Your Inner Child Holds the Keys to Alignment

"When you laugh, the field expands. When you play, the gate opens. Joy is a portal—step through it."

You know how kids can play with a cardboard box for hours and be completely fulfilled? That's divine power in motion. That's imagination flexing its muscle. That's creation without pressure. And you still have access to that power—if you're willing to let go of the grown-up grip and play again.

Play isn't childish. It's spiritual technology. It's one of the fastest ways to shift your frequency from force to flow.

Joy lifts your vibration. Laughter loosens stuck energy. Silly moments—freestyle dancing, cartoon voices, pillow fights, chasing bubbles—bring you back to your natural state: open, curious, magnetic, alive.

When you're stressed, trying too hard, or overthinking the outcome, play breaks the spell of control. It sends a signal to the quantum field:

"I trust. I receive. I create freely."

Scientific Insight: Joy and Dopamine Flow

Play triggers the release of dopamine, oxytocin, and serotonin—brain chemicals responsible for pleasure, trust, and relaxation. This shift in neurochemistry expands your creative capacity, reduces cortisol (the stress hormone), and creates a neurobiological environment ideal for manifestation.

In short: when you play, you unlock higher states of consciousness.

Universal Law: The Law of Least Effort

Aligned creation doesn't come from stress—it flows from trust. This law reminds us that ease attracts more than effort alone. Play is the path of least resistance, and that's where miracles flow. When you're in joy, you're not chasing—you're allowing.

Personal Experience

There was a day I was spiraling in overwhelm—trying to figure out how to solve too many things at once. Bills, business, book writing, healing. It was all too much.

Then one of my nephew's children came in, handed me a toy, and said "Let's play."

For a moment, I resisted. I got things to do! But something told me—this is the thing to do.

We giggled. We made silly noises. I let my hair down.

And I kid you not, later that night, a major breakthrough came.

A financial door opened. A conversation I'd been waiting for arrived. My energy was different. I wasn't tight—I was tuned in.

That's when I got the download:

"Joy is a frequency opener. Play is a portal."

Ritual: 5-Minute Joy Reboot**

Use this ritual when your energy feels tight, serious, or over-controlled.

What You'll Need:

- A playful item (toy, music, bubble wand, funny video, silly hat, etc.)

- 5 minutes and no shame

Steps:

1. Set a timer for 5 minutes.

2. Choose a playful act: goofy dance, humming a theme song, coloring with crayons, impersonating a cartoon, skipping around the room.

3. Laugh. Smile. Be present in the absurdity. Let go.

4. After the timer goes off, place your hand over your heart and say:

   "My joy is holy. My play is powerful. I am now aligned with ease."

Journal Reflection:

What activity made you feel joyful and free as a child—and how can you bring a version of that into your adult life?

Affirmation:

"Play is my portal. Laughter is my ladder. Joy is my alignment—and I rise with it daily."

Volume I – Chapter 8: From Wishing to Manifesting – Quick Guide Companion

Section 3: Frequency First Aid Kit – What to Do When You're Out of Alignment

Subtitle: Instant Tools to Shift Your Energy and Reboot Your Day

"You're not stuck—you're just staticky. And baby, we've got tools for that."

Sometimes you wake up off.

Sometimes the vibe just nosedives out of nowhere.

You catch an attitude. Your energy dips. Nothing seems to flow. And that old voice whispers, "It's all falling apart."

Pause. Don't spiral. Don't shame yourself.

Just know this: you're not broken. You're out of alignment.

And just like tuning a radio, you can shift your signal.

That's what this Frequency First Aid Kit is for—those moments when affirmations feel fake, the journal's too far, and you just need a reset now.

Scientific Insight: Energy Disruption and Nervous System Regulation

When your energy drops, it's usually a sign of nervous system dysregulation. Stress hormones spike, the brain defaults to survival mode, and your frequency contracts. But with simple sensory cues—sound, breath, movement, scent—you can bring the body and energy field back into coherence. That's neurobiology. That's quantum.

Universal Law: The Law of Perpetual Transmutation of Energy

This law states that all energy is in motion and can be transformed. Even the densest, lowest vibes can be alchemized into higher frequency with intention. You have the power to transmute—instantly.

Personal Experience

I used to think I had to wait until I "felt better" to raise my frequency. But now I know—I don't have to feel my way into action. I can act my way into frequency.

There've been days I was in the gutter emotionally, but the moment I opened the window, danced to a song, or said one single loving thing to myself, I felt the shift. Sometimes the shift is subtle. Sometimes it's massive. But it's always possible.

Your Frequency First Aid Kit

Use any of these when you're feeling low, cloudy, cranky, or disconnected. Mix, match, stack them as needed.

- Move Your Body: Shake your arms, jump, stretch, twerk—movement resets stagnant energy.

- Sonic Reset: Play a song that instantly lifts your mood (have a playlist ready).

- Breath Bomb: Inhale for 4, hold for 4, exhale for 8. Repeat 3 times.

- Water Reset: Drink a full glass of water slowly. Or splash cold water on your face with intention.

- Name the Vibe: Say out loud: "This isn't who I am—it's just what I'm feeling. And feelings move."

- Light + Smell: Light incense or use essential oils (peppermint, citrus, lavender).

- Sun Hit: Get outside for 2–5 minutes. Face the sun. Say "I receive."

- Quantum Flip: Say "Reset. Realign. Restore." as a command to your field.

Mini Ritual: Emergency Frequency Reset

Use this 90-second practice when you can't think straight or feel emotionally scrambled.

Steps:

1. Close your eyes and place one hand on your chest, one on your belly.

2. Take one slow breath and whisper: "I am safe. I am here. I am recalibrating."

3. Open your eyes, stretch your arms, and say aloud:
   "Shift made. I am back in alignment."

4. **Journal Reflection:**

What tends to throw off your energy the most—and what's your new go-to reset from the kit?

Affirmation

"I shift with grace. I rise with tools. My energy is mine to command—and I reset with love."

Volume I – Chapter 8: From Wishing to Manifesting – Quick Guide Companion

Section 4: Inner G Reflections – Daily Journal Prompts for Self-Realization

Subtitle: The Questions That Unlock the Quantum You

"The answers you seek are already inside you. All you have to do is ask the right questions."

You don't need to be a monk on a mountaintop or a guru with a crystal ball to receive divine guidance.

Sometimes all it takes is one good question.

One honest moment.

One mirror held up to your mind.

That's what Inner G Reflections are about. These aren't just journal prompts—they're activation codes.

They help you get clear on who you are, where you're stuck, what you truly want, and how to course-correct with power, not pressure.

Because manifestation is less about making stuff happen, and more about making yourself ready to receive it. These questions will help clear the clutter, call your energy back, and bring your inner God(dess) online.

And you don't have to write pages. One sentence in truth is louder than five in performance.

Scientific Insight: Journaling and Emotional Integration

Journaling strengthens the connection between the emotional and logical centers of the brain. It activates the prefrontal cortex (executive function) and helps process complex emotions, reduce anxiety, and improve memory recall. It's not just therapeutic—it's neurological organization. Writing helps you rewire.

Universal Law: The Law of Self-Creation

You are not just a byproduct of your past—you are the author of your Now. Every reflection, every realization is a step toward conscious creation. To know yourself is to wield your power.

Personal Practice

Some of my deepest breakthroughs didn't come from a book or a video—they came from me asking myself questions I used to avoid.

- "Why does this still trigger me?"

- "What part of me is scared to shine?"

- "Am I being loyal to my potential—or my pain?"

And whew, the answers?

They weren't always cute. But they were healing.

Because even when I didn't know the full solution, I had finally gotten honest. And honesty is the GPS of transformation.

Inner G Reflection Prompts

Use these as morning tune-ups, bedtime downloads, or mid-day realignment tools:

- What's one belief I need to release to receive what I'm asking for?

- If my frequency created today's experience, what was I vibrating?

- Where am I hiding my light out of habit or fear?

- What part of my inner child still needs validation today?

- What would my highest self do differently in this exact moment?

- What do I need to forgive in myself to rise fully?

- Am I watering weeds or planting vision with my thoughts today?

- What am I afraid might happen if I actually succeed?

- What's one loving thing I can say to myself right now?

- If my soul had a voice, what would she say to me this second?

Ritual: Inner G Mirror Moment

Use this when you're ready to look yourself in the soul and hear what needs to be heard.

What You'll Need:

- A mirror (handheld or bathroom)

- A timer or your breath

- Your full presence

Steps:

1. Stand or sit before the mirror.

2. Choose one Inner G prompt from above. Ask it aloud or silently.

3. Look into your own eyes for one full minute. Don't look away.

4. Say aloud whatever comes up—even if it's "I don't know."

5. End by saying:
   "I see you. I love you. We're evolving together."

Journal Reflection:

Which Inner G prompt hit the deepest nerve—and what came up when you sat with it?

Affirmation

"I reflect to evolve. I question to grow. My truth is my tool, and my clarity is a sacred spell."

Volume I – Chapter 8: From Wishing to Manifesting – Quick Guide Companion

Section 5: The Power Fist – 5-Finger Affirmation Reset

Subtitle: Grab Your Frequency Back with One Hand

"Your hand is a wand. Your words are weapons. Your fingers? Five codes of command."

Sometimes you don't have time to write, meditate, or break out the sage.

Sometimes you're in the car, in a meeting, in the shower, or just in a moment—where you need a fast, fierce reminder of who the hell you are.

That's when you ball up the Power Fist.

This isn't just a gesture. It's a ritualized reset.

Your five fingers become five affirmations.

Your clenched fist becomes a declaration.

It says, "I'm reclaiming my mind, my vibe, my frequency—right now."

This is for those days when you feel fragmented. Small. Shaky.

Or when you just need to tighten up the vibe and stand firm in your field.

The Power Fist is spiritual CPR for your consciousness.

Scientific Insight: Hand Gestures, Neuroassociation & Embodiment

Research in psychology and kinesiology shows that physical gestures enhance belief and memory retention. When you pair movement with affirmation, your nervous system locks it in deeper. The clenched fist signals power and resolve—triggering physiological responses that increase adrenaline, focus, and confidence.

You're not just saying the words—you're embedding them into your body.

Universal Law: The Law of Command

The Universe responds to clarity and conviction. When you speak with command—not fear, not begging, but authority—you become a co-creator, not a wish-maker. You are not hoping—you're declaring.

Personal Practice

I created this when I was at a breaking point—tired of the back-and-forth inside my head.

I stood in the mirror, closed my eyes, and without planning, I clenched my fist and said five things out loud.

It wasn't pretty. It wasn't poetic.

But it was powerful.

And every time I do it now, I feel my field realign.

It's simple. It's fast. It's free. And it works.

The Power Fist – 5-Step Affirmation Ritual

Here's how it works. You say one affirmation for each finger, then seal it with the full fist.

Do this anywhere, anytime. No tools needed. Just you.

1. Thumb – "I am safe."

   (The foundation. Nothing sticks if you don't feel safe.)

2. Index Finger – "I am guided."

   (The pointer. You're not lost—you're divinely directed.)

3. Middle Finger – "I release what doesn't serve."

   (Yup, that one. Release with boldness. You

don't owe struggle your loyalty.)

4. Ring Finger – "I am worthy of receiving."

   (Commit to yourself like a sacred vow.)

5. Pinky Finger – "I trust the timing."

   (The smallest reminder often holds the deepest faith.)

6. Full Fist – "And so it is."

   (Seal it. Own it. Activate it.)

Mini Ritual: Emergency Power Lock

Use this version for extra reinforcement before a difficult conversation, interview, decision, or if you wake up in a low-frequency loop.

Steps:

1. Hold your open hand in front of your chest.

2. Speak each affirmation out loud while folding each finger.

3. Once the fist is closed, hold it to your heart and whisper:

"This is my field. This is my truth. And this is my command."

4. Take a deep breath. Exhale like you mean it.

Journal Reflection:

Which of the five affirmations do you resist the most—and what deeper belief might be hiding underneath?

Affirmation:

"My hand is a signal. My words are a shield. I reset, realign, and rise—in power, purpose, and peace."

Volume I – Chapter 8: From Wishing to Manifesting – Quick Guide Companion

Section 6: Body Technology Hacks – Breathwork, Mudras & Power Poses

Subtitle: Activate the God-Code in Your Flesh

"Your body isn't just a vessel—it's an instrument. Every pose is a prayer. Every breath is a reset button."

Your body is not separate from your spirit—it's your sacred technology. A bio-electric, frequency-transmitting, manifestation-activating man-chine.

And guess what?

It has built-in keys for energy alignment.

When you shift your posture, you shift your power.

When you move your breath, you move your reality.

You don't need a crystal or a sage bundle (though they're dope too).

Sometimes all it takes is a hand gesture. A stance. A deep inhale.

The ancient ones left us clues in the body—and it's time to remember them.

This section gives you quick physical tools to unlock presence, power, and peace—using what you already carry.

Scientific Insight: Posture, Hormones & Bioenergetics

Studies by social psychologist Amy Cuddy and others show that "power poses" increase testosterone (confidence hormone) and lower cortisol (stress hormone) in just two minutes. Breathwork regulates the vagus nerve, which shifts you from fight-or-flight into rest-and-receive mode.

Hand mudras stimulate nerve endings and organs through neuromuscular signaling—literally telling the body to enter a new energetic state.

Universal Law: The Law of Embodiment

You can't just think higher—you have to embody higher. This law reminds us that manifestation doesn't just happen in the mind. It flows through the body, breath, and posture. When you stand differently, you attract differently.

Personal Practice

I remember being in a moment of chaos—my mind racing, emotions all over. I couldn't think my way out.

But I stood tall, took one deep breath, and held my hand in a simple upward mudra. I felt a shift.

Not because I solved everything—but because I told my nervous system:

"We are safe. We are divine. We got this."

And sometimes, that's the breakthrough.

Body Technology Hacks

Use these anytime to reset your field through the flesh.

Mudra: Gyan (Wisdom Seal)

Gesture: Touch tip of index finger to thumb, other fingers extended

Use for: Clarity, wisdom, mental stillness

Say: "I am clear. I receive divine instruction."

Power Pose: Victory Stance

Pose: Arms raised in a wide V, feet grounded, chest lifted

Use for: Confidence, embodiment, command

Say: "I stand in victory. I rise with purpose."

Breathwork: 4-7-8 Reset

Inhale for 4 | Hold for 7 | Exhale for 8

Use for: Stress, overthinking, nervous system balance

Say on exhale: "I surrender to peace."

Mudra: Kubera (Manifestation Seal)

Gesture: Press index, middle, and thumb together

Use for: Focused intention, wealth attraction

Say: "I receive exactly what I envision—multiplied."

Pose: Boundary Lock

Pose: Arms crossed over chest, palms flat on shoulders

Use for: Energetic shielding, sovereignty

Say: "I choose what enters my field."

Ritual: Full-Body Frequency Lock-In

Use this when you want to embody your next level, fast.

Steps:

1. Stand tall, feet hip-width apart.

2. Inhale deeply and lift your arms in the Victory Pose.

3. Exhale slowly, bring hands to heart in prayer.

4. Hold Kubera Mudra and say aloud:

   "I lock into divine alignment. My body is my amplifier. I radiate power, peace, and purpose."

5. Repeat once more while looking in the mirror.

Journal Reflection:

How have you been holding your body—and what new stance or breath would reflect your next level?

Affirmation:

"I carry divine intelligence in my bones. I move like I am guided. I stand like I am chosen. I breathe like I already won."

Volume I – Chapter 8: From Wishing to Manifesting – Quick Guide Companion

Section 7: Sound Healing Shortcuts – Quick Sonic Tune-Ups

Subtitle: Let the Frequencies Do the Fixing

"You don't have to fix it—just tune it. Sound carries what words can't reach."

Sometimes your energy is too jumbled to journal.

Too tired to talk it out.

Too overwhelmed to "figure it out."

But you still need a shift. A clearing. A reset.

That's when you let sound do the work.

Sound doesn't need your permission. It doesn't need your logic.

It goes straight to the nervous system, the cells, the bones, the aura.

It slips past the ego and sings directly to the soul.

This is why ancient cultures used drums, chants, bells, bowls, mantras, and flutes. Because sound has always been a tool of healing, cleansing, and divine remembrance.

You don't have to "understand it."

You just have to feel it.

Scientific Insight: Cymatics & Frequency Healing

Cymatics is the science of sound made visible. When frequencies are played through a medium like water or sand, they form geometric patterns—proving that sound literally shapes matter.

The human body is over 70% water, which means every vibration you hear is forming a new pattern inside you. Specific frequencies (like 528 Hz for DNA repair or 432 Hz for peace) have measurable effects on heart rate, mood, and cellular harmony. Sound = vibrational medicine.

Universal Law: The Law of Resonance

You don't attract what you want—you attract what you resonate with. Sound healing shortcuts help you quickly shift your resonance so your field matches what you actually desire. Vibe first. Manifest second.

Personal Practice

There've been moments I couldn't speak what I was feeling. My words were stuck. My thoughts were racing. But when I laid down and let a singing bowl hum across my body—or when I let a sound bath wash over me—tears came. Then clarity came. Then calm.

It was like my cells exhaled.

No explaining. No processing. Just releasing.

I left those sessions feeling reorganized, like my inner system had been reset back to divine code.

Now, when I feel out of tune, I don't force clarity—I press play on the right frequency.

Sound Healing Shortcuts You Can Use Daily

Use headphones, speakers, or hum it out loud. Trust the sound to do the lifting.

Tuning Fork or Singing Bowl

(esp. near the crown, heart, or solar plexus)

Use for: DNA recalibration, chakra cleansing, deep calm

Frequency: 528 Hz or 432 Hz

Say: "I allow this sound to return me to harmony."

Voice Humming

(close your eyes and hum into your chest)

Use for: Nervous system reset, emotional release, self-soothing

Say: "My body receives my own healing tone."

Mantra or Chanting

(e.g., "OM," "Ra Ma Da Sa")

Use for: Focus, spiritual alignment, vibrational clearing

Say: "My voice is a tuning fork for my divine field."

Frequency Music

(YouTube/Spotify: "432 Hz," "963 Hz," "Alpha wave meditation")

Use for: Background tuning while working, sleeping, driving

Say (inwardly): "I am being recalibrated in real time."

Ritual: Sonic Aura Rinse

Use this when you feel energetically "dirty" or heavy from a space, person, or emotional crash.

What You'll Need:

- Frequency track (432 Hz, 963 Hz, or healing bowl playlist)

- Headphones or speaker

- A quiet or dim space

Steps:

1. Sit or lay down. Close your eyes.

2. Play the sound and imagine the frequencies pouring over you like water.

3. With each breath, visualize static leaving your field.

4. Say softly:

   "I am tuned. I am cleared. I am recalibrated."

Let the sound do the work. Don't think—just feel.

Journal Reflection:

What's one sound, song, or frequency that immediately shifts your mood—and how can you use it with more intention?

Affirmation:

"Sound is my healer. Frequency is my medicine. I realign with every note and rise in every tone."

Volume I – Chapter 8: From Wishing to Manifesting – Quick Guide Companion

Section 8: Energetic Shielding – Quick Protection for Empaths & Sensitive Souls

Subtitle: Guard Your Field Like It's Sacred— Because It Is

"Being empathic doesn't mean being exposed. Sensitivity is a superpower—but it needs spiritual boundaries."

You ever walk into a room and instantly feel drained?

Ever talk to someone and feel like you inherited their whole bad day?

Ever leave a conversation and wonder why your vibe crashed?

If so, you're not crazy—you're picking up spiritual residue.

And if you're an empath, intuitive, or just vibrationally open, you already know this world is loud. Heavy. Full of subtle tugs on your peace.

But here's the good news: You can protect your field.

You don't have to absorb what's not yours.

You don't have to walk around raw and rattled.

With simple energetic tools, you can set boundaries without being rude, shield your aura without being cold, and keep your compassion without being depleted.

Scientific Insight: Electromagnetic Fields & Human Biofields

Your body emits an electromagnetic field—especially from the heart and brain. This "aura" has been measured by instruments like magnetocardiograms, proving that your energy radiates feet beyond your skin.

Sensitive people simply feel those fields more acutely. But when you set intention, use visual cues, or ground your nervous system, you can stabilize your frequency and stop unwanted energy from sticking.

Universal Law: The Law of Correspondence + Law of Boundaries

"As within, so without." Your internal boundaries reflect your external ones. If you believe you're unprotected, you'll attract situations that drain. But when you claim sovereignty, the Universe respects it.

Energetic boundaries are a form of self-love—and they teach others how to treat your field.

Personal Practice

I used to walk through the world like a sponge— soaking up people's emotions, sadness, chaos. I thought being "spiritual" meant being always available. But that left me depleted, moody, and confused about what was mine and what was theirs.

Now? I shield my energy like it's currency.

I learned to say:

"I'm not cold. I'm covered."

"I'm not rude. I'm reserved for what aligns."

My field is no longer public property.

And I've never felt more powerful.

Energetic Shielding Shortcuts

These are tools you can use in seconds—no crystals or rituals required (but feel free to add them).

Visual Shielding

Close your eyes and imagine a golden light bubble or mirror field around you.

Say: "Only love enters. All else reflects away."

Smell + Sense Grounding

Use lavender, sandalwood, or frankincense oils and inhale slowly.

Say: "This scent seals my peace. I call my energy back to me."

Body Seal (Cross-Arm Technique)

Cross your arms across your chest.

Exhale through your nose and say:

"My energy is sealed. What's mine stays. What's not returns."

Voice Shield

Whisper or say aloud before entering a space:

"I do not absorb what isn't mine. I remain sovereign in every room."

Vortex Spin (Advanced)

Visualize a clockwise swirl of wind or light spinning around you, removing residue.

Say: "I spin off what's not aligned. I emerge clear and charged."

Mini Ritual: Daily Field Seal

Use this each morning—or before interacting with heavy energy.

Steps:

1. Stand or sit tall. Place both hands over your heart.

2. Breathe deeply and visualize your aura glowing like soft gold.

3. Say aloud:

   "I am shielded in light. I am grounded in truth. I am protected, aligned, and divinely covered."

Repeat after exposure to dense spaces or toxic interactions.

Journal Reflection:

Where do you tend to give away your energy the most—and what boundaries are ready to be set?

Affirmation:

"I guard my frequency like treasure. My energy is protected, my presence is powerful, and my spirit is sovereign."

Volume I – Chapter 8: From Wishing to Manifesting – Quick Guide Companion

Section 9: The 2-Minute Mental Garden Clean-Up

Subtitle: Weed Your Thoughts. Water Your Vibration.

"Every thought is a seed. Some grow weeds. Some grow wonders. Choose wisely."

Your mind is a garden, and your thoughts are seeds.

Some sprout peace, confidence, clarity.

Others? Doubt, anxiety, shame.

And just like in any real garden, if you don't pull the weeds, they'll take over.

This 2-minute clean-up is a mental reset ritual for when you realize you've been spiraling into negative loops—whether it's fear, comparison, overthinking, or straight-up self-doubt. You don't need to spend an hour journaling. Just notice. Weed. Replant.

This isn't about being perfect.

It's about being present.

Catch the weed before it chokes your frequency.

Scientific Insight: Thought Loops & Neuroplasticity

Negative thought patterns carve grooves in the brain, reinforcing emotional and behavioral responses. But due to neuroplasticity, your brain can rewire with repetition and intention. Every time you interrupt a negative loop and replace it with a new one, you're literally reshaping your mind.

Universal Law: The Law of Mentalism

Everything begins in the mind. Thoughts become things because consciousness precedes creation. What you mentally cultivate becomes the soil from which your life grows. Mind your mental garden, and manifestation follows.

Personal Practice

I used to let one negative thought bloom into a whole damn forest. One "what if this doesn't work?" would turn into, "I knew I wasn't ready," and suddenly I'm doubting my entire destiny.

Now? I do regular garden checks.

I ask: "Is this thought a weed or a seed?"

If it's a weed—I pull it.

If it's a seed—I water it with belief.

I don't argue with negative thoughts anymore. I just stop feeding them.

2-Minute Mental Garden Clean-Up Practice

Use this when you catch your vibe slipping into negativity or when self-doubt creeps in.

Step 1: Catch the Weed

Ask: "What thought just made me feel heavy, anxious, or off?"

Don't judge it—just name it.

Step 2: Pull It Gently

Say out loud:

"This thought doesn't serve my growth. I release it now."

Step 3: Plant a New Seed

Replace it immediately:

Old thought: "What if I fail?"

New seed: "What if this is exactly how I win?"

Step 4: Water It

Say it again—but this time like you mean it.

Feel it. Own it. Smile at it. That's watering the vibe.

Done. Garden cleaned. Field reset.

Journal Reflection

What recurring "weed" thought do you need to retire—and what new "seed" thought are you planting in its place?

Affirmation

"My mind is fertile ground. I plant only what feeds my future, and I pull what no longer belongs."

Volume I – Chapter 8: From Wishing to Manifesting – Quick Guide Companion

Section 10: Closing Mantra – Sealing Your Field Before Sleep or Social Settings

Subtitle: Wrap Your Energy in Light Before the World or the Dreamworld

"You lock your doors at night. Lock your aura too."

Your energy field is real—and it's porous.

Throughout the day, it brushes against people, spaces, screens, timelines, and even astral activity while you sleep.

So why wouldn't you seal it?

This isn't fear-based. It's frequency-based hygiene.

Before you walk into the world—or drift off into dreamland—you can wrap yourself in energetic light, affirm your sovereignty, and command your field with love.

A closing mantra is like spiritual armor made of vibration.

You don't need a full ritual. Just a few words. Full presence. Strong intention.

That's the code.

Scientific Insight: Sleep, Brainwaves & Subconscious Programming

As you fall asleep, your brain enters theta and delta states, where the subconscious is most programmable. What you feed it in those final waking moments becomes part of your internal code.

The same applies to high-stimulus social situations. Your nervous system scans for safety, and the field becomes vulnerable to absorption. Speaking a closing mantra activates your parasympathetic system and reinforces energetic protection.

Universal Law: The Law of Intentionality

Whatever you do with focused intent creates a ripple in the field. A small act—like a whispered mantra—can shift your entire frequency trajectory. Rituals create rhythm. Rhythm creates results.

Personal Practice

There've been nights I crawled into bed heavy with the weight of other people's energy. And I'd wonder why I woke up tired. It wasn't just the body—it was my field, unsealed and unguarded.

Now? Before sleep or crowds, I seal my field like I seal an envelope—with care, clarity, and command. And I rest like a goddess wrapped in light.

Closing Mantras to Use Anytime

You can whisper these before sleep, after prayer, before entering crowded places, or anytime you want to protect your energy and stay aligned.

For Sleep:

"I close this day with grace. I call my energy back to me, and I release what is not mine. My field is sealed. My rest is sacred. My spirit is safe."

For Social Protection or Public Energy Fields:

"I am sovereign in every space. My aura is sealed with light. Only love and alignment may enter. All else dissolves."

For Emotional Closure (after intense conversations, sessions, or scrolling):

"I release what I've absorbed. I return to center. I close this loop and return to wholeness."

Mini Ritual: Aura Lock-In Before Sleep

Use this each night before bed or nap time to anchor your sleep in peace.

Steps:

1. Sit or lie down comfortably. Close your eyes.

2. Visualize a soft light cocoon wrapping around your body—any color that feels safe.

3. Breathe in deeply and say:

   "I am whole. I am home. I am held."

4. Say your chosen closing mantra three times. Let the final one echo into silence.

5. Drift into sleep—or back into life—sealed in sacred vibration.

Journal Reflection:

What energy do you want to take with you into sleep—and what do you need to let go of before you rest?

Affirmation:

"My energy is sacred. My field is sealed. I rest in protection, and I rise in power."

Volume I – Chapter 8: From Wishing to Manifesting – Quick Guide Companion

Section 10: Closing: Your Spiritual Inheritance Is Already Yours

Subtitle: You Don't Have to Earn What Was Always Written in Your Name

"You don't audition for what's in your bloodline. You don't compete for what's already yours. You simply receive it."

You don't have to fix yourself to be worthy.

You don't have to pray harder, do more, or hustle for heaven.

You're already chosen.

Let's be clear: this isn't about ego.

This is about inheritance. And inheritance, by definition, is something passed down to you simply because of who you are.

Not what you've done.

Not how perfect you've been.

Not what title you carry.

You are here. You are divine. And you have a spiritual trust fund with your name on it.

It's coded into your DNA.

It's waiting in your field.

It's already yours.

What Is Spiritual Inheritance?

Spiritual inheritance and the core meaning of inheritance of being worthy of something simply because you exist and the concept of you don't have to do anything to be valuable or deserve it. You don't have to perform a task to be worthy of receiving your inheritance because it's yours simply because you exist, and you are valuable and deserving of it simply because you exist.

It's the unconditional birthright of every soul to receive love, abundance, peace, wisdom, joy, intuition, protection, guidance, and divine connection.

It's not earned through perfection. It's not performance-based. It's not gatekept by religion, titles, or trauma.

It's simply what you carry by being made of God-stuff.

You are the descendant of Source.

You are the continuation of creation.

And that means—you don't have to qualify for the blessing.

You just have to claim it.

Scientific Insight: Worthiness and Cellular Programming

Studies show that people with a sense of deservedness and belonging have stronger immune systems, lower cortisol levels, and higher manifestation success. Why? Because when the body believes it is safe to receive, it opens the pathways for healing, connection, and quantum attraction.

Worthiness isn't just emotional—it's energetic permission.

Universal Law: The Law of Divine Right

Everything that belongs to you by divine blueprint cannot be blocked when you remember it's already yours. The Law of Divine Right affirms that no one—not even your past self—can stop what God assigned to your spirit.

Your job isn't to fight for it.

Your job is to stop disqualifying yourself from it.

Personal Reminder (from Me to You)

There were times I thought I had to "do more" to deserve peace.

To grind harder to earn joy. To look holier to be considered chosen.

But then I realized: I already was the thing I was trying to become.

The blessings I was begging for were written into my soul contract the day I took my first breath.

You don't need to change to be worthy. You don't need to suffer to be blessed.

You don't need to prove your divinity. You are the proof. You are the gift.

You are the inheritance and the heir.

Ritual: Receiving What's Already Yours

Say this out loud. With breath. With knowing. With zero hesitation.

"I don't have to earn what I already carry.

I am not waiting to be chosen. I was born chosen.

I activate my spiritual inheritance now. I open my arms to receive, not to beg.

I rise because it's written. I walk as the heir to divine goodness.

It's already mine."

Journal Reflection:

What would change in your life today if you fully believed you already had the blessing?

Affirmation:

"I am not applying—I am already appointed. My inheritance is divine, and I claim it in full."

Arrival

Poem

It's a dog eat dog world, it's a sport, who got the Most heart

I feel like mentally, me and earth are worlds apart,

Past galaxies, moons and stars

How I got here? I'ma rewind it from the start.

It took a minute to arrive, now that I'm in it; I'm soo glad I made it out alive.

I pried the door open, to open the hearts and minds wide

I've tried to be the nice guy, and let niggas slide,

I sat background, so I wouldn't hurt, y'all niggas pride.

So the nay-sayers, would have a false sense, my Skillz have died.

Now its go-time, cuz it's show time, I knuckle up for the rhyme.

I'm a gold mine, this whole time, So Buckle up for the ride.

I'm coasting thru the cosmos, on battleship Galactica.

Taking the universe by force, I tackle it, I'm smackin' ya,

on the black hand side, wit tha Mic still in hand

The keeper of the gold, steel vault my brand

Harping on the fact, I orchestrate my own fate

There have been too many times, I thought I was gonna break

I got God's downloads, guidance and defiance, for negativity.

I chuck tha deuces to my high fivin' enemies,

They would cringe to see, my lineage royalty, but it's still no reason to envy me

Exposing my blood is not the remedy, they hatin' hard enough already.

When jealousy precedes, reality's perception, it's hard to see who I really be, genuinely.

Past the cool exterior, custom style,

Flow's superior and chestshire smile,

My spitfire's wild like the joker I am

With more raw sex appeal, than a villainous bad man,

Bustin' thru doors, only cuz I'm a Ram

Those are just perks, but it's not all of who I am.

So allow me to re-introduce myself ...

Daughter of Jo-Jo, Sister of Yummy, grew up broke but now I gets money,

Well ... On that ever exhausting paper chase,

Either you standing on the sidelines or you get in the race.

Empty pockets and Empty mouths keep me on my feet.

I got hella people in my family, plus me, and we all gotta eat.

I internally struggle wit Ego vs G-O-D

Strivin' to get from high end pauper, to permanently VIP.

The industry, got haters and wack niggas, gassed I see

I'll walk up to a fake nigga, like…let me see your ID

Personally, wack niggas are like farts, I think.

They ain't shit, They just stink.

I sat back for too long, and witnessed the injustices on stages,

From so called freestyle to written in pages

But far and in between, have I seen the true passion.

They're just spitting, for ghetto recognition, for they poetry\rappin'.

I don't be askin', for much just a fraction

of how I give it- Mo' thriller, than Mike Jackson,

So haters can just beat it, if you care about your
survival.

I fall through the spot, like a falsetto High Note

Coming in late, but right on time, feeling good and
looking fine

Fake asses, pay false compliments, but really they can
keep it

It sounds like gibberish, they don't get it, I don't need
it

Haters be mad, cuz I practice my craft

I'm forged in fire, you don't know half of the half

You can't calculate the cost, cuz most them niggas was
bad at math

The hate be like octane for me, it fuels my gas

There's more ILLA in me, than Godzilla .

So poised and classy but I keep it soo Trilla.

My method, man is to bring the pain.

Addicted to the flow like liquid cocaine.

I got credentials coming out my asshole.

From tours, colleges, articles

and magazines. basically anything I could grab hold.

Mark my territory upon arrival.

Nothing to prove, allodial is my title

Made many loyal comrades, and die-hard rivals, from all tribals.

Both groups propel me to greatness, my wave is tidal,

I'm compelled by the pen, first off, cuz without it I'd be worse off

It's my anger management, when tempers burst off.

And it's my way to get the dirt off.

I won't join the rest, raking in green with pants down and shirts off.

U gotta wiggle low, society's an American jiggalo,

Nigga's know, the world is filled, with pimps and hoes.

There's always some Pro's, trying to take advantage.

I pivot positions, keep my head on swivel, to manage the damage

It forces me to stay on my toes, like a ballerina.

I sit back, and laugh at rat cats, like a hyena,

My mind ain't from this planet.

You ask, do I still have it?

God gave it, so of course I still got It,

Me to lose, naw son stop it.

True I know my worth and yes I profit,

But I'm not in it for the profit but to be a prophet

and deliver downloads and testimonies of black
power, love, and struggle,

Ranting, raving, misbehaving, and the hustle,

Self-help and whatever else, to share me, naked and
vulnerable

To touch spirits, through poetic lyrics, under my
hardness, I'm really lovable.

I can only be me to the truest,

With my left-I throw up tha west, and yes, I grew up
in that part of St. Louis.

Youngest of 6 from moms and papa was a rolling
stone,

Definitely he couldn't be alone with several homes

So I'm 1, of a large international team

Product of a southern belle and a Nigerian Idi Amin.

I mean at times it seemed, that mama grew mean,
from daddy's antics,

And punishments were drastic,

Me and Sis would plan tactics,

and wished we had magic to practice

To get tha fuck up out of there.

Abracadabra and Disappear into air.

Had kidnapped siblings, God knows where

With pops in Africa, him ruling with fear.

But we didn't understand that as kids

We were left with a biased mother, that beat asses and put chains around the fridge.

That's just 1 stop along my way, you can see the marks, from the tire skids

My life filled with all kinds of other things, ... but I lived.

So fast forward to this moment right here,

I pummeled thru the pain and tears

And I've arrived to this point and conclusion

You're just a product of your experiences, your healing and your bruising.

And just so there's no confusion

When I shine, it's a byproduct of fulfilling my purpose, not spark insecurity

If you're in your feelings, it's just a lack of maturity

Haters let me tell you like this, if you don't like it

There's a soft part of me, you can lay your lips on and kiss.

I'm too grown and been thru too much

To take any stance other than "And So Muthafuckin' What"

So keep talking, but keep watchin', you're bound to catch an eye-full

Like UFO spacecrafts, I invade upon arrival.

by Idara Umana/ILL SkillZ 5-14-08

Work Sick

Poem

Phone alarm, ringin already, it's time to get up.

Go to this, dream deferred distraction Damn! I'm hit in the gut

Fill my cup, make a few buhhhcks.. and run it uhhp.

Work to eat meals, and pay bills, to sum it up

What the fuhhck! In my bed, my eyes red

...Am I really going? I got a side bet

Explain to a client, What I'm, gonna freakin say?

Excuses, run 'round like riots, in a hundred different ways

Just thinking all that shit, got my head hurting now.

Beefing that its milking, like a ...herd of cow.

Not high off the hog, more like a ..dirty sow.

This job.. shit.. is working. How?

Shits hard keepin' my pockets well endowed

Got me mad tight, like a night, with a virgin's vow.

This version now of life, I end this chapter

Turn the page NOW, not a second after

Scream from rafters, Universe be my backer!!

Got billion dollar gifts, from a poet to an actor

Tempted to stay in bed, talk ME off the ledge.

But I gotta wakey bakey and get to the bread.

Rise to the occasion, gotta get fresh and clean

Meditate in the steam, quantum jump to my dream.

Baptized completely with my new future.

Crystallize, marry my thoughts, like I'm a suitor.

Jobs be dogging me, so I'mma get it neutered.

Got time to make up, sew the game up like sutures.

Mental bullets, I shoot ya -snipe ya from a tower

As soon..as I..get out.. the shower.

As soon..as I..get the power to quit.

To be honest with me, I've had enough of it.

Yo yo yo I'm so work sick, Yo yo yo I'm so work sick

No, no, no it's not worth it

Now is the time, I'm gonna live my purpose

If ain't workin, I'm in pain, sick or hurt

Simply sick of working, and that's the worst.

The rains gone..sky's as clear can be.

It's clear to me this aint the life, meant for me.

Fly somewhere. Yeah! Change the scenery

Weed, palm trees, water, greenery

A vacay, to stay, play, detached from it all

When it's time to go back, I get ghost, and don't call

Mentally checked out, and I ain't even there yet

On my way to the top and I leave on LearJet

Settle for less? What for? Taking no more L's

Worked my own mess...a little personal hell

Yeah I get money, eatin' hard, I bite my fingers

You can tell, the way I move, it's all in my demeanor

Life's coffee, you know, I gotta have the cream

See me sliding in the streets, but shit ain't what it seems

I'm work sick! My only cure's to Go HAM!

Give no fucks, no damn, to any sir, no ma'am,

Born to lead...I'm on Mars with a Ram cuz

I'm Red carpet ready with stars and cameras

I'm off the leddddggge...Made a leap of faith

I believe so much in me, that's the risk I'll take

Back on my throne, to do what I'm born for

Overthrow, strip the Emperor's clothes he wore

This means war...on being work sick

My plans perfect, a wordsmith, with my verses

On my jerk shit, yeah, it's time to be selfish

Can't help it! All them years gone and I felt it

Overcame obstacles that had to be dealt with

Claw my way to the top, from a barrel of shellfish

Yo yo I'm so work sick, Yo yo I'm so work sick

No, No, No, it's not worth it

Now is the time, I'm gonna live my purpose

I'mma fight for this shit, square up in real bouts

Industry wants me to be iced and chill out

But I'm too hot to handle when I'm bringing ILL out

Turned the deal down, hoe cards was only dealt out

It's hard to bait a shark- They brought the reels out

Now I'm healed up, yeah, bust open sealed mouths

There's a casting couch, Me Too with this

Cloak and dagger, with the swagger...no witnesses

Quietly ...side eye viewed me as little fish

Ain't think, I'd come back to sip tea and dish

Can't get away holding my dream hostage

I'm GAY, so No Thanks, on Rec Exec sausage

Passed days where bosses, fuckin' the whole office

The cost is your art and your pride is your losses

Fuck dat shit!!! ...I had to take a step back

Fall back, on other gifts, Yeah I'm charging a tax

Yeah, these are the facts!

Fall back on other gifts, Yeah, I'm charging a tax

Hustling, self employed...Here and There jobs

Settling for less than JOY ...so I felt like a fraud

Since how it played out, I went hard on Plan B

When your dreams deferred, to get back infinity

To do what I do its cool...but it's really not Me

If I was with the Fuck Shit, then I would be Top 3

Straight poppin, not slutting out, so don't knock me!

Yeah I talk my shit...cuz all eyes dot Me

Cursed with Work sick, but I found the Cure

Expand me in the world, start there for sure

Endure, immerse, embrace my REAL LIFE

Take my piece of the pie, I make sure it's real nice

Got nothing to left lose, every right to gain

Speeding to my destination, on a bullet train

Derailed, now on track, I get it back in bags

The size of trash, not Berkin...and I get it real fast

Retire from the J-O, I really gotta go go

No monkey business here, got the mojo like jojo

I power puff on platforms, change to impact

Shakin' norms, take by storm, nothing left intact

In fact, today's the day, I'll be the first to admit

I did all kinds of shit...to get really rich

Nothings my passion...so it never really sticks

After I make a few dollars, shit...I be ready to quit

To be honest this job shit...you can have all of it

Dreams smoke like incense...yet I burn like phoenix

Got fires to light bright...YES! my shit be intense

I QUIT! I'm feeling better.. from being WORK SICK!

ILL Skillz 1-4-23

Final Affirmation

*I am a living transmission of truth, a vessel of divine
remembrance.*
*Every page I turn, every truth I speak, every scar I survived was
sacred.*
I am not just an author—
I am the spell, the spellbreaker, and the spoken word of God.
This is my calling.
This is my legacy.
And it is already written.

Volume I Glossary: From Cotton Fields to Quantum Fields

Affirmation

A spoken or written statement that programs the subconscious with intentional frequency. A tool for shifting thought patterns and aligning the vibrational field with desired realities.

EMF (Electromagnetic Field)

Invisible waves of energy that interact with the body's bioelectric system. Excessive EMF exposure from devices can cause energy depletion, which may require spiritual or physical rebalancing. The invisible frequency net around the body that picks up thoughts, emotions, and influences from others. When polluted with negative thoughts, it distorts manifestations and attracts chaos. Must be cleared regularly through breath, visualization, or spiritual hygiene.

Energy Vortex

A swirling energetic field created intentionally or naturally, used to restore personal power and alignment. Breathing exercises, hand spirals, and visualization activate this vortex to reclaim drained life force.

Epigenetic Rewiring

The scientific and spiritual truth that beliefs, thoughts, and environment change your biology. When you visualize your future self vividly and consistently, you change the chemical code of your cells—and thus, your entire life.

Ineffable

That which is beyond words or explanation. A sacred truth so powerful, so deeply known in the soul, that it cannot be fully spoken—only felt.

Journal Prompt

A reflective question posed to the reader to provoke self-inquiry, healing, and personal transformation based on the teachings of the chapter.

Mudra

A hand gesture or position that channels specific energy flows through the body. Often used in meditation, manifestation, and energetic alignment.

Paradigm

The invisible program running in the subconscious, shaped by belief, culture, and trauma. A paradigm is the lens through which reality is filtered—until it is rewritten.

Quantum Field

The invisible matrix of energy that surrounds all matter. Thoughts, emotions, and frequencies influence the field to create outcomes. The field responds to feeling, not just words.

Ritual

A sacred action or symbolic act meant to focus energy and intention. In this book, rituals serve as tools to seal each teaching and help the reader embody the wisdom.

Shadow Work

The process of exploring and integrating hidden emotions, beliefs, and traumas that influence your behaviors and energy. It's a pathway to healing, self-acceptance, and ascension.

Spiritology

The sacred study of spiritual science, vibrational mechanics, divine psychology, energetic technology, and inner alchemy. A metaphysical system of understanding the inner and outer cosmos as one continuous truth

Universal Law

The invisible governing principles of creation, such as:

- Law of Vibration: Everything moves and emits frequency.

- Law of Correspondence: As within, so without.

- Law of Mentalism: All is mind. The universe is mental.

- Law of Cause and Effect: Every action has a corresponding reaction.

Yoga Breath

Conscious breathwork used to regulate energy, clear emotional blockages, and activate the divine engine within. Often used to reset the nervous system and transmute negative thought patterns.

Spiritology Glossary: Original Language of the Inner G

Inner G

A divine force within each person—your inner guidance, God-force, generator, and genius. It's the metaphysical battery that animates, instructs, and powers your thoughts, emotions, and manifestations.

Backseat

A metaphysical state where the SubC has taken full control. The conscious mind is silenced. The person becomes a passenger in their own life—reactive, confused, and often unaware of their own divinity or direction.

Default Program

The automatic pattern of response written by past experiences, media, trauma, family, and society. If unexamined, it becomes fate. If reprogrammed, it becomes freedom.

Divine Playpen Principle

A metaphysical teaching that Earth is a spiritual playground where souls evolve through experiential learning. God acts as the divine parent allowing safe exploration, joy, and transformation.

Flawed Messenger

The idea that divinely chosen vessels need not be perfect—flaws, pain, and humanity are part of what make the messenger relatable, powerful, and real. They have lived enough life to understand the messages that flow through them.

Frequency

Not just sound—it's your mood, your vibe, your setting. It's the dial you're tuned into. You manifest what matches your frequency, not what you wish. That's why guarding your radio dial (thoughts + music + emotions) is sacred.

Frequency Thief

An energy-draining person, device, or system that disrupts your vibrational harmony. Can include phones, toxic people, environments, or even your own subconscious beliefs.

God Power

The inner access point to divine creation energy within all beings. When aligned with thought, speech, emotion, and intention, it allows a person to become a conscious co-creator of reality.

Man-chine

The divine fusion of man and machine—referring to the human body as a bioelectric vessel running on spiritual software. When the mental program (mind) is aligned with the quantum field (God), the Man-chine becomes limitless. A blend of man and machine.

Refers to the human body as divine technology, equipped with circuitry, intelligence, and energetic mechanics, powered by thought, breath, and spiritual will.

Power 5 Fist

A sacred mental phrase or affirmation repeated during moments of stress, temptation, or reprogramming. It disrupts old neural pathways and installs new beliefs. Best used with conscious breathwork to seal new intention into the nervous system. A concentrated affirmation set focused on 5 core vibrational alignments: Identity, Clarity, Protection, Purpose, and Love. Designed for daily recitation to establish sovereignty and divine resonance.

Sacred Sleep Window

Also called The Golden Time of Night. The hour right before sleep and immediately upon waking, where the subconscious is most programmable. A prime time for planting intentions and divine downloads.

Spellcraft

The conscious use of language, tone, and intention to influence energy. Recognizes that all speech is vibrational casting—either aligning or misaligning your field with your desires.

SubC (Subconscious)

The shadow speaker. The bodyguard of your soul. It stores emotional memories, trauma responses, chemical addictions, and reactive behaviors. When untrained, it will run your life on outdated programming. When guided, it becomes a powerful ally in manifestation and protection.

Tell-I-Vision

You, as a vessel of sacred information and visionary truth. A play on "television"—a spiritual antenna that transmits divine downloads for humanity's evolution.

The Mental Garden

The inner landscape of the mind, where thoughts are seeds. The SubC is the soil. What you water grows. Weeds (unprocessed trauma or toxic programming) must be uprooted to allow divine crops to bloom. Conscious attention is the gardener, and beliefs become the harvest. Your reality is a reflection of what is planted and nurtured.

Wild Child of the SubC

The untrained, reactive, pop-culture-programmed inner voice that curses, panics, distracts, or sabotages your evolution. Can be funny, emotional, or defensive—but needs spiritual parenting, not suppression.

12-Second Yoga Breath

A breathing technique to silence the subconscious hijacker. Breathe in 4 seconds, hold 4, release 4. Used to calm the nervous system, stop emotional spiraling, and reset the energetic field to a divine vibration.

Captain & Vessel Analogy

The Conscious Mind is the captain.

The Body is the ship.

God is the wind, stars, water, and compass.

Your job is to steer with intention, not drift in default mode.

About the Author

Idara Umana is a divine vessel, a truth-teller, and a walking revelation. Poet, Actor, Lyricist, now Author. Born of ancestral brilliance and forged through trials, she is a master storyteller, metaphysical teacher, and poetic architect of vibration and vision. Her work is rooted in lived experience, sacred downloads, and a bold commitment to collective healing—especially for the marginalized, the misjudged, and the misunderstood.

Idara channels spiritual insight through rhythm, wordplay, and raw honesty. Her journey has taken her through both suffering and sovereignty, and she now uses every page as a portal to remembrance, revolution, and rebirth.

This is not just her book—this is a **frequency transmission**. A call to rise. A permission slip to remember.

Connect with Idara

- **TikTok:** @TheRealiLLskillZ
- **Email:** wordjewelry.illskillz@gmail.com
- **#FromCottonToQuantum**
- **Publisher:** Illumanate Entertainment LLC

QR Codes for Quick Link

Go Fund Me- To help My Family that was severely affected by the St. Louis Tornado of 2025.

A portion of the proceeds from this book will be donated to support those affected by the devastating 2025 tornado in St. Louis, Missouri— particularly the underserved communities hit hardest by the storm. I LOVE MY CITY.

My YouTube Channel- Word Jewelry

TikTok- @The Real ILL Skillz

Gratitude

To my family, loved ones, friends, and soul supporters—thank you for believing in me, even when I was still becoming.

To every client who sat in my chair and let me style more than just your hair—thank you for the exchange, the energy, the trust.

To every food customer who tasted my seasoning, felt my spirit, and came back for more—you were feeding more than a business, you were feeding a dream.

To my community, my readers, my chosen family—your love is legacy.

To my haters… thank you. You were unexpected teachers.

Your resistance only sharpened my frequency and deepened my alignment with purpose.

To **God**, to the **unseen ancestors**, and to my **divinely tuned inner channel**—you are the Source of all that flowed through these pages.

Every epiphany, every breakdown, every breakthrough, every sacred download…

I heard you.

I trusted you.

And I obeyed.

This book is not just a product of my hands.

It is a manifestation of my soul.

Thank you to everyone who played a role in awakening it.

www.ingramcontent.com/pod-product-compliance
Lightning Source LLC
Chambersburg PA
CBHW060256150626
46556CB00021B/14